BOBBY FISCHER

BOBBY FISCHER
THE WANDERING KING

Hans Böhm and Kees Jongkind

B T BATSFORD

First published in the Netherlands by
Tirion Uitgevers BV in 2003

Published in the United Kingdom 2004

ISBN 0 7134 8935 9

A CIP catalogue reference for this book is available from the British Library

Translated from the Dutch by Kaarlo Schepel

Printed in Great Britain by
Creative Print and Design (Wales, Ebbw Vale)
for the publishers
B T Batsford
The Chrysalis Building
Bramley Road
London W10 6SP

A member of Chrysalis Books plc

Contents

Introduction

The sports division of the NOS (Netherlands Broadcasting Foundation) started a new TV series at the beginning of 2003: 50-minute documentaries about exceptional sportsmen and sports events. Bobby Fischer, official chess World Champion in 1972–75, living legend and man of extremes, also became a subject. Fischer appeals to the imagination of the chess world because of his crystal-clear games and inspiring determination to win; to the outside world, Fischer completely conforms with the image of the mad genius. This documentary, *The Wandering King*, was shown on 14 January 2003. Because Fischer is not someone who will happily discuss his own life in front of the camera, he is presented as others see him. Korchnoi and Benkö tell about the whims of Fischer in 1962 and afterwards. Hans Ree talked with Fischer in 1968 about Jewry and Israel. Harry Sneider still sympathizes with his friend Bobby Fischer, whom he helped in the difficult phase around 1972. Max Euwe testified to great organizational impediments just before the match in 1972. Lothar Schmid and Hans Böhm remember Fischer during his triumphal procession in Reykjavik that year as if it were yesterday. Anatoly Karpov regrets that his match with Fischer in 1975 did not take place. Arnfried Pagel tried to snare Fischer for his chess club in 1980. Jan Timman went to the pub with Fischer in 1990. Dirk Jan ten Geuzendam brought Fischer information about Spassky in 1992 in a Yugoslavia in flames. Yasser Seirawan talked for a whole day with Fischer about all and sundry during his match in 1992. Zsofia Polgar peeled potatoes in Budapest with house guest Fischer somewhere around 1995. Nigel Short is almost certain that in 2001 he played against Fischer on the internet. Eugene Torre arranged for a woman to carry Fischer's baby in 2000, and said in late 2002 that he had little contact anymore. Jaap van den Herik looks from 2003 back into the time when Fischer made fun of the chess computer.

Many dozens of hours of raw material, collected in interviews from all over the world, had to be reduced in the end to less than an hour for our broadcast. Choices had to be made for a larger public than just the chess public. This book makes its own choice from that footage. You will read the most striking insights about, and experiences with, Bobby Fischer. What is striking is that everyone, friend and foe alike, speaks with a mixture of both respect and horror.

This respect is not only based on Fischer's phenomenal chess accomplishments; his one-man struggle against the entire Russian chess establishment cannot be overestimated. Fischer also invented a digital chess clock because of his displeasure with the shortcomings of the mechanical clock. From the sand dipper, by way of the chronometer and then the double mechanical clock (invented by Thomas Bright Wilson and used for the first time in London in 1883), Robert James Fischer presented in 1992 the next revolutionary stage – the Fischer clock – which today is used at all levels of chess play. Fischer has further proposed a new starting position for the pieces, displeased as he was with ever-increasing knowledge of opening permutations. In Fischer Random Chess the pieces stand on the lowest ranks in an opening position that is determined by computer for each game. All the advantage of current theoretical knowledge would be cancelled by it, and as a result, a player's pure chess power can conquer once again. This innovation is being tried out sporadically here and there (the second Fischer Random Chess World Championship was played in Germany in July 2004, with many top grandmasters participating). Fischer also managed to raise the payments and conditions of professional chess players in general significantly, by sacrificing his own material – and immaterial – interests.

The horror relates to the changes Fischer's character underwent since he became the best player on earth in 1972 – which is to say from the moment the sobering effects of reality stopped being applicable. Those character changes are comparable to the manner in which a committed revolutionary sometimes degenerates when he becomes absolute ruler. In radio interviews – which do not deserve to be called interviews because Fischer is allowed to express his frustrations uninterrupted – always the same subjects are on offer: the American government forced him wrongfully in 1992 to go into exile; there is a worldwide Jewish conspiracy, which is behind the auction of his Pasadena storage space and its valuable memorabilia; he is still owed millions in royalties for books, movies and the Fischer clock; the classic form of chess is dead; and all Russians cheat.

Fischer may magnify reality in his line of reasoning to absurd proportions, creating fire-spitting monsters with nine heads and a hollow laugh. His life story, however, shows the real events behind the birth of these little monsters. Fischer *was* shadowed by the FBI, the KGB *did* have a Fischer file, the Russians *did* conspire against Fischer, Fischer *did not* get all the royalties to which he was entitled, and the auction of his storage space *was* wrongful.

In this book, full use is made of the FBI files that became public in December 2002, five years after the death of his mother Regina Wender. The *Philadelphia Inquirer* was the first to lay hands on the FBI file, with documents from 1942 to 1972. It also becomes apparent that the man Fischer regarded as his father, Hans Gerhardt Fischer (who married Wender in 1939), was not his biological father, who was a man named Paul Nemenyi. Bobby Fischer was the son of two very intelligent and headstrong parents.

In *The Wandering King,* KGB documents that have come into circulation since the fall of communism in Eastern Europe are also quoted. Fischer was considered an important object of study, it seems, up to the highest levels.

Bobby Fischer surprised the world from 1949 to 1972 with his talent for chess. In 1972, at the pinnacle of his career, he stopped abruptly. In 1992, he played once more in a remarkable return match against Spassky, and after that Fischer never played again. But whether Fischer now plays chess or not, everything newsworthy he does is instantly reported in the media. That is what happens to living legends. The May 2002 issue of *New in Chess* says about the following about Karl Rove, George W Bush's top strategist:

> 'And what do these journalists invariably call him? What wondrous epithet is bestowed time and again on this loyal and generally admired patriot? That's right, you will find it hard to find an article in which Karl Rove is not called "the Bobby Fischer of American politics"!'

The examples are legion and in all languages, and they will continue to appear. 'Bobby Fischer' still stands for an intelligent, clear strategy and an extreme determination to win, even if he has not played chess for almost thirty years.

Acknowledgements

In order to be able to see all stories about Bobby Fischer in the right perspective, we elected to view his life from a bird's-eye angle. For this purpose, the extensive archives and expertise of the Max-Euwe centre in Amsterdam were consulted, and well-known author of chess idiosyncrasies Tim Krabbé was approached as a source as well. I had a great time with Tim in Reykjavik in 1972, and Fischer has refused to let go of either of us ever since. Through Fischer's website at home.att.ne.jp/moon/fischer/ you will have access to all radio interviews, photo material and articles by and about Fischer. I wish to thank the rating officer of the Royal Netherlands Chess Federation (KNSB) for his sensible suggestions. Also cordial thanks to anyone who sent us material, whether or not it eventually proved useful. The responses to our requests clearly show how Fischer still appeals to the imagination.

Bobby Fischer turned 60 in 2003. Let's hope that he will pick up chess again somewhere in the future. The title 'best senior of all times' can be claimed for the moment by Emanuel Lasker (1868–1941) and Viktor Korchnoi (born 1931), who at age 70 is still counted among the best 50 chess players of the world.

I have the uncanny feeling that if Fischer, for whatever reason, would just decide to sit down behind a chess board, he would immediately play the stars from the sky. We sports editorial staff at the Netherlands Broadcasting Foundation have in the meantime tried to let Fischer tell his own story.

Hans Böhm

The Making of *The Wandering King*

The idea of making a documentary about chess legend Bobby Fischer had something exciting and mysterious about it from the very start. Fischer is a name from another age. How is he doing? Where is he now? What is he up to? Those kinds of questions were immediately asked when the proposal was put on the table during a meeting of the Studio Sport documentaries work group.

This little group was created after Gerard Dielessen joined the NOS as head of sports in 2002. Naturally, we concentrated in the first place on reporting sports events, but there is room for other, longer-term projects. Making documentaries belongs to that category.

In January 2003, we were going to broadcast three documentaries in a new series, Studio Sport Document. Two of these were cooked up in our own oven, while the third – about Dutch boxing champion Regilio Tuur – was purchased from an outside producer. The list of potential subjects was large, but in the end, it was decided that one of our in-house programmes would be a portrait of Rinus Michels, the most famous Dutch football trainer ever, who was then turning 75. The theme of the other special (a term we prefer to 'documentary', a word laden with unwanted associations) would be the adventures of Bobby Fischer.

The idea actually arose because Youri, the son of our colleague Maarten Nooter, had a school speaking assignment to do on Fischer. As 'junior' began to dig into the eccentric American's background, Maarten's long-hidden memories of the legendary match in Iceland in 1972 began to surface. His resulting enthusiasm at our next meeting was so contagious that we began to ask ourselves the questions mentioned above: How is he doing? Where is he now? What is he up to?

Together with editor Jurgen Leurdijk, I occupied myself from the start above all with collecting information about Fischer. The internet is an inexhaustible source for this. We who are in our thirties of course knew that he had become world champion in 1972 by beating Spassky in Iceland, and we could also remember that he had made himself impossible by playing chess once more in Yugoslavia during the civil war, against the same opponent. But that was just about it.

As we started out, we immersed ourselves with astonishment in all the stories that had been written about Fischer, about his youth, about his neuroses, about his radical opinions, about his behaviour, about his anti-Semitism. We quickly arrived at the conclusion that we were dealing with a nut. Fischer also has his own website on which he uses abusive language against everything and anyone he does not like, and on which he tries to prove that the property removed from his storage space in Pasadena was stolen by 'the Jews'.

You may question why Dutchmen would be interested in an American chess player who disappeared. The game is popular in our country only among a limited circle of people. The masses would probably prefer a beautiful portrait of, say, an ice-skater. We nevertheless decided to carry on with our project, because it excited us so much and because we were convinced that viewers might be carried along by this absolutely insane story.

The challenge was to depict the person of Fischer accurately, with all his abhorrence for the Russians, his anti-Semitism and eventually his hatred against America. Besides these aspects, we wanted to set his story in a historical perspective. After all, he was part of the Cold War; he was the American hero who destroyed the chess army of the Soviet Union all by himself. It not only earned him the freedom of the city of New York. Now, more than thirty years later, he has changed into a vindictive schizophrenic who spoke enthusiastically to a Filipino radio audience about the two planes that tore through the Twin Towers.

The third path we took was the search for Fischer himself. Naturally, we wanted to find him in Japan, where he currently lives. We were dreaming of a man with a long beard, wandering about in a Japanese supermarket. We would approach him quite casually: 'Are you Mr. Fischer?' He would look at us and see that we were good people, from that decent Dutch television station. He would invite us to come back to his place, and after he had asked his geisha to kindly leave the room, he would give us more than hour-long answers to all our questions and we would happily go back to Hilversum with tapes full of useful material. DREAM ON!

There is almost no useful picture material of Fischer. It was therefore an enormous challenge to locate images and pictures of him from the past. Granted, the NOS has a very extensive library of sports images, but the name of Fischer does not appear in it. The newsreels indeed had images of that controversial match in Sveti Stefan in 1992, including when he spat on the American government order forbidding him to play there. We further found in the broadcasting library a tape of a splendid broadcast by Teleac (the Dutch public education channel) presented by Max Euwe from Reykjavik during the match with Spassky in 1972. We were sitting and cheering in front of the screen when suddenly the camera moved through the press room and ended up focusing on two chess-playing hippies. It was easy to identify the first one as Dutch writer Tim Krabbé. The other one was an almost unrecognizable Hans Böhm, with long hair and an enormous unkempt moustache. Hilarity all around!

Both gentlemen were approached by us to cooperate on the special. By this point we had decided to let others tell the story, because the chance that we would be able to record Fischer in person was small. The criterion was that our interlocutors must have met Fischer in the flesh. That applies to both Krabbé and Böhm, who were witnesses of the world championship in Iceland. The former sent a short e-mail with the message that he had already written a book and many other stories about Fischer and that he did not really have anything to add to these.

Böhm however was enthused. Jurgen Leurdijk and I spoke with him in a Hilversum restaurant. We then discovered for the first time what kind of emotions Fischer brings about in chess players. After a few introductory stories, Hans started to tell us about the very last game in Reykjavik. It had been adjourned, and next day it became apparent that Spassky had resigned by phone. When the rather awkward, tall Fischer appeared on the podium, chief arbiter Lothar Schmidt pronounced him the winner. The public embraced the

American with a deafening applause which Fischer did not know how to handle. He just stood there, shy. Böhm told us that he joined wildly in the applause, as a way of honouring Fischer's entire works as a chess player. The applause continued to break in waves over the new world champion, and Böhm felt as if it should never have stopped. When talking about it a very small tear escaped from the corner of his eye. With the carelessness gesture, he wiped the moisture away and took a drink.

Before we started filming, Jurgen and I also visited Jan Timman in Amsterdam. The nice thing about Jan is that he is capable of placing Bobby Fischer in all imaginable historical contexts. I shall not easily forget the meeting: the whole apartment was full of laundry and unopened mail and we had to do our very best during the conversation to shout louder than Bob Dylan, whose singing accompanied our interview in the background. My appreciation of Timman increased tremendously that morning. He lives the existence of a chess player as I have always visualized it.

We got utterly exhausted sending e-mails and making telephone calls while looking for people who could give us information; to experts who could give us a better insight into the mythical Fischer through their stories. Remarkably, not everyone was jumping at the chance to appear in front of a camera. We found out that the inner circle surrounding Fischer did not say a word, because if he finds out that anyone he knows has talked to the press about him, it instantly means the end of their friendship. A well-known story is the one told by Ron Gross, a friend from his youth. He told a journalist in his innocence that he and Fischer had gone fishing together. That was then quoted in the article. He discovered that he was not a friend any more after that.

We tried to reach Ron Gross, but he had apparently learned his lesson. William Lombardy, the faithful second in Iceland, does not want to say anything about Fischer either. 'He is keeping his memories to himself,' according to an e-mail from Alaska.

The silence surrounding Fischer is deafening. His family keeps silent too. Fischer's mother, sister, and a cousin all died over a period of five years. The only family members left are his brother-in-law Russell Targ, who lives in Palo Alto, and Russell's sons Alexander and Nicolas. They did not want to cooperate.

The few chess friends that Fischer has did not see any purpose in talking either. The Yugoslav grandmaster Svetozar Gligoric said no, and so did Boris Spassky. Spassky's refusal was a major disappointment; he should not have been absent from the programme. We finally solved this problem by purchasing a previously existing interview from Icelandic TV. In this way we shopped around among a variety of broadcasting organizations, from Russia to America, from Yugoslavia to Iceland. If we disregard the fact that looking in picture archives is very time-consuming, this shopping tends to be especially expensive. A number of programmes were made in the past about the confrontation in Reykjavik. The BBC's *Clash of the Titans* and Arte's *La guerre des échecs* (The Chess War) are two documentaries that we viewed with a great deal of interest. The BBC had managed to lay its hands on black-and-white footage of a very young Fischer giving a simultaneous display in New York and analyzing a position on the board. But it turned out that those pictures were not the property of the BBC; the producer had bought them from another picture archive – which no longer existed. We finally traced it to a company called Einstein TV. In this manner we gathered the entire special – frame by frame.

In the Arte documentary, fragments of the first game in Reykjavik could be seen in colour. The Fox company wanted to make a movie about the match in 1972 and had set up various cameras in the playing hall. But they had to put these back in their cases after the first game, because Fischer blamed his loss on the noise the equipment made. Where did the footage of that first game go? We found out through the French that APTN in London was now the owner of the pictures, but NBC in New York had another two minutes of other material. We had everything sent to Hilversum, and it was indeed splendid material. We could even see Fischer making the fatal move that lost him the game.

We also did some filming ourselves. A committee member of the Bobby Fischer junior chess club in The Hague suburb of Wassenaar had kept a scrapbook about his hero in his youth. This was of great value because of the newspaper headlines and photographs. Chess on the internet, in order to illustrate the story of Nigel Short, was recorded by us in the attractive chess café Gambiet on the Bloemgracht in Amsterdam.

Through the editors of the *Nova* programme, we got in touch with a Dutch camerawoman in New York. She filmed the apartment at 560 Lincoln Place where Fischer grew up. That is not a nice neighbourhood these days, so her driver kept the engine running as she filmed. She also filmed the exterior of Erasmus High, Fischer's high school. One of his classmates there was Barbra Streisand. Her management never responded to our request to interview her about the chess player.

We are happy to say that there were still people who were willing to appear in front of the camera, and one of them belonged to the circle of

Fischer's friends. Harry Sneider, the fitness trainer from Pasadena, who helped Fischer's physical training and who is still a good friend of his. He was convinced of our good intentions. He considers it a tragedy that Fischer started to behave more and more strangely, and he used our request as a way to call on his friend to start playing chess again. Sneider told Meindert van der Meulen, our enthusiastic producer on the spot, how Fischer lived after he suddenly stopped playing chess in 1972 and retired into the anonymity of the Worldwide Church of God.

In this way, through more than a dozen interviews, we wanted to paint a picture of the life, the actions and the thoughts of Bobby Fischer.

Together with cameraman Peter Bijlmakers, I made an international journey among the various Fischer experts. Several times we asked ourselves what strange kinds of characters these were. It started straight away in the first interview, with Arnfried Pagel in Berlin. He became very rich by owning the rights to a certain type of concrete, and for 25 years he lived in Bergen aan Zee, where he established a chess club: the Koningsclub (King's club). He went to Pasadena in order to try to convince Fischer to come and play chess in the Netherlands.

I had been warned in advance by all kinds of people in the chess world that Pagel would be a dreamer. Indeed, he told such an unlikely story about his meeting with Fischer that Peter and I afterwards doubted his credibility. That doubt was reinforced when he claimed to have had photos of himself and Fischer, but that they had been lost in a fire. We nevertheless included Pagel in the programme, even if only to indicate what kind of fantastic stories were told about Fischer. You can read extracts from the interviews with Pagel and the other experts later on in this book.

In the neighbourhood of Frankfurt, we met Lothar Schmid, the chief arbiter of the tournament at Reykjavik. Schmid eloquently told us of the problems that the match organizers had experienced with Fischer, and about his cooperation with Max Euwe, with whom he succeeded in steering the match for the world championship in the right direction.

In the Netherlands, we interviewed Dirk Jan ten Geuzendam, chief editor of the chess magazine *New in Chess*. Fischer had asked him in 1992 to come to Sveti Stefan with the entire record of the Spassky games. Miraculously, he was able to produce the fax in which he was asked to come to Montenegro, signed by Bobby Fischer.

Hans Ree is the only Dutchman still alive who ever played Fischer. We interviewed him in the Max Euwe museum in Amsterdam. There in a glass display case is Fischer's scribbled note in which he resigns his game with

Donner. A real museum piece. We had to disappoint the exceptionally kind staff member of the centre who told the story behind that piece of paper with conviction; these shots didn't make the final programme.

I had never seen hundreds of people play chess at the same time, but I have to say, it was an impressive sight. At the beginning of November 2002, the chess Olympics were held in Bled, Slovenia. The enormous congress centre was completely filled with chess players from all over the globe. The absolute top was also present, and some of them have their own experiences with Fischer. The British player Nigel Short told us about his belief that he played against him on the internet. The American grandmaster Yasser Seirawan recalled his meeting with Fischer in 1992. Seirawan and his Dutch wife Yvette Nagel were granted – just like that – 11 hours with the master. The valuable part was that they were allowed to ask him whatever questions they wanted. Fischer told them about his youth, about the Russians, about his anti-Semitism, about his hatred against America, and against the international chess federation. In this way we got to know a lot about the thoughts that make Fischer tick.

We also tried to have a conversation in Bled with the Filipino grandmaster Eugene Torre. He is considered to be one of Fischer's most loyal friends, and even for a long time provided him with a roof over his head in Baguio City. In view of our earlier experiences with Fischer's friends, we approached Torre while he was unaware he was being filmed. Torre kindly listened to me, but when he understood that I wanted to interview him about Fischer, he backed out.

We of course wanted to draw Gary Kasparov into our story. He was the top member of the Russian team during the Olympiad. Everyone we asked for tips about the way to approach him blanched at the thought. 'What? Are you guys going to approach Kasparov? Watch out, he can be very nasty.'

Jurgen had contacted Owen Williams, the American agent of Kasparov, to be on the safe side, but we got little response, so we just decided to risk it. The ex-world champion had a day off, which might be to our advantage. Peter and I kept watch for a while in the hall of the players' hotel. The plan was that I would first ask Kasparov politely for an interview before Peter would grab his camera.

He came down around lunchtime. I jumped up, stretched out my hand: 'Mr Kasparov, I'm working for NOS TV from the Netherlands…' He immediately released my hand and snarled: 'So what?' While I was making another attempt to explain exactly for what reason we were there, he had already turned away: 'Bye, bye.'

Jurgen called a bit later from Hilversum. He had just received an e-mail from the manager of Kasparov: 'You should be aware that Mr Kasparov usually steers clear of anything involving Mr Fischer because of his erratic behaviour in recent events, especially the live radio interview in Budapest.'

It is not surprising that Kasparov did not want to waste a word on Fischer, because the latter had depicted him as a filthy liar who meticulously prepares his games. This tirade was, by the way, heard not on Hungarian radio, but in Iceland. The mistake was logical, as Fischer had aired his opinion of Kasparov on various radio stations in the past few years. He meticulously keeps track of these on his own website, where the 20 radio interviews can all be heard in their entirety. We also contacted Icelandic radio and Radio Bombo in the Philippines. How do you get an interview with Fischer? The rules are simple: he only does radio, he will only appear live (so that his words cannot be edited), he cannot be interrupted, and the broadcasting company cannot be 'managed by the Jewish mafia'. Through the Icelanders we got two e-mail addresses for Fischer in Japan. One of them started with US-IS-SHIT@. That had to be Fischer. We exhausted ourselves in making attractive proposals in a vain attempt to seduce him into talking with Dutch television. The result: no reaction whatsoever.

We were also active in Japan. Wanted: a large, heavyset, white man with a beard. He was bound to stand out among all those Japanese. But our contacts in the Land of the Rising Sun could not find a thing. An editor of a TV programme that traces missing people could not find anything either. Not a single paragraph seems to have been published in the Japanese press that the ex-world champion was even living there. Nothing.

Fischer made hiding for the outside world an art. In 1985, William Nack of *Sports Illustrated* searched for him in the vicinity of San Francisco for 21 months. He knew that Fischer frequented libraries. Nack made it a habit to go every day to a different library hoping that he would run into Fischer. His plan eventually succeeded when he suddenly stood eye to eye with the vanished grandmaster: 'I ducked behind the card catalogues and leaned my head against the files and said in a suppressed whisper: "Oh my God! I found him! I don't believe this. Now what the hell do I do?" '

Nack did not know how he should react, or what he should say. He decided to follow Fischer. But once out in the street, Fischer moved into fifth gear, crossed the road, jumped on the first bus that came by, and disappeared. Nack can at least say that he really saw the myth alive, even if it was for just a moment.

We had nothing else left but to let others tell the story. What are the books that Fischer is promoting? We found David Barnouw of the Netherlands Institute for War Documentation prepared to review *The Secret World Government* by Count Cherep-Spiridovitch. How is it possible that people see a Jewish conspiracy behind everything ? The American vents his hatred against the Jewish people and the Americans in all his recent radio interviews. Even supposing that we had found him, and he had been willing to talk to us, the chances would have been high that we would not have been able to broadcast the material. What a bunch of sordid stories.

As a young man he had a violent dislike of the Russians. That could at least be explained, because three Soviet chess players had played games with him during the Candidate tournament in Willemstad, Curaçao, in 1962. During the chess event in Curaçao in November 2002, that earlier memorable tournament was extensively reviewed.

The confrontation during the 2002 opening ceremony between two players of that previous era, Viktor Korchnoi and Pal Benkö, was magnificent. Master of Ceremonies Hans Böhm only had to add a bit of oil to the fire and the two of them, along with Yuri Averbakh, one of the Russian trainers, soon got into an argument. There were clearly past scores that had not yet been settled. Petrosian, Geller and Keres, it seems, had conspired against the rest. They drew against each other so they could concentrate their energy on playing the others. This is the basis of Fischer's suspicion against everything Russian.

Willemstad was the perfect background against which to view the complications of forty years earlier. Pal Benkö, a Hungarian-born American, admitted that he quarrelled with Fischer at the time. Their friendship had since been restored, but he could not help us to get into contact with the American. But Benkö had a piece of news: Fischer had supposedly been married in the meantime, and had a child.

The meeting with Viktor Korchnoi was a tremendous experience. He is now in his seventies and is still a real fanatic for chess. He lost to Zsofia Polgar during a lightning chess event on that Sunday afternoon. A shame! 'This is the very first and the very last time you have won a game against me in your life,' he barked at the Hungarian.

Korchnoi is the angry old man of chess. He has developed an enormous dislike for Fischer because the latter alleged in 1992 that all Russians made deals among themselves. Korchnoi does not let that pass; he became so fed up talking about Fischer that he broke off the interview himself. 'I do not wish to talk about Fischer any more.'

Hans Böhm and Jan Timman really took the time to tell us about their experiences with Fischer. And finally, Zsofia Polgar, in whose parents' house Fischer was a regular guest when he lived in Budapest, came to the conclusion that she is not at all happy she ever met him.

Once back from the Netherlands Antilles, Jurgen was on my voicemail. Anatoly Karpov was about to make a stopover in Amsterdam on his way to New York. He could be interviewed in his hotel. That was a tremendous piece of good luck; the man who succeeded Fischer as world champion was lavished upon us.

In the end all the interviews, the material from the archives and the radio fragments were pieced together, and were made into this 50-minute special, *Bobby Fischer: The Wandering King*. The reaction from viewers was exceptionally positive. But the story had a small sequel.

After the broadcast I had a call from a Dutch businessman who does business in Serbia. He had seen a Yugoslav business associate of his in the pictures of the match in Montenegro. This Mr Michailovic was supposed to be a good friend of Fischer, and still in daily contact with him. He could possibly arrange an interview with him for us in Tokyo. Would this be the golden tip? We called Belgrade straight away. Indeed, Mr Michailovic not only was an acquaintance of the chess player, he also had an appointment with him in Japan. He would do his best on our behalf.

Weeks passed. The telephone line with Serbia remained silent. He did not call, he did not e-mail, and whenever we got him on the phone, the time was inconvenient and we had to call back later.

Still, just before the Americans invaded Iraq, we unexpectedly got an e-mail from Fischer himself. Slightly excited, we opened the message. Was it an invitation for an interview? Of course not. We got 'important' news about the US Defence Secretary:

> 'The cat is out of the bag! U.S. Secretary of Defense Donald Rumsfeld is a f**king Jew. Thanks and have a good day.'

The king continues to wander.

Kees Jongkind

Part I

1943–1972
The Rise of a Chess Genius

Robert James Fischer

Who is the chess player who speaks most to the imagination of all time? If the number of books that were written about an individual are the most important indication, then Fischer will be the greatest of all chess players of the last 1500 years, since the game of chess was invented. Fischer inspired many people both as a chess player and as a person. More than 30 books appeared about his 1972 world title match with Spassky in Reykjavik alone. A small sampling from the library: Fischer's youth, Fischer as prodigy, Fischer on a tour of simultaneous displays, lightning games by Fischer, all games of Fischer, Fischer's results against Russian players, Fischer's loves and lovers, Fischer's handwriting, the riddle of Fischer, Fischer's special moves, Fischer: the greatest?, Fischer's disappearance, Fischer's return, 'the unknown Fischer'. His entire life has been described in many languages. And even when Fischer disappears from the limelight and does not touch a chess piece, he inspires. In 1993, the movie *Searching for Bobby Fischer* came out after the book of the same name. The hand-written final sentences which appear just before the lights go out look as if they have been glued on afterwards: 'In September 1992, Fischer broke off his isolation in order to challenge his old rival Boris Spassky. When he had won, he at once disappeared again.'

In 2003, on the occasion of his 60th birthday, not a single chess magazine failed to dedicate a fine nostalgic editorial to the phenomenon of Fischer. The NOS made the documentary on which this book is based, in which others sketch an image of Fischer; Fischer himself prefers to remain untraceable. His life story is told in many ways and sketched in many colours, but the feelings of friend and foe agree on two aspects: how that man could play chess! And what a terrible pity that his career developed the way it did.

The parentage of Robert James Fischer alone is a difficult subject of study. His surname could just as easily have been Wender or Nemenyi. FBI files were publicly released only recently (after the usual 30 years), from which it is apparent that the organization first followed Fischer's mother for a long time (and meticulously), but later also her son (see FBI Files, page 135). The *Philadelphia Inquirer* was the first to put its hands on the files by means of a Freedom of Information request. Fischer's mother Regina Wender was suspected of spying for the Russians. In view of her previous history, this was not a completely outlandish possibility. Regina came from a red background. She was born in 1913 in Switzerland, of Polish-Jewish parents. After her family emigrated to the United States, she grew up in St. Louis, and after she got her bachelor's degree at the University of Colorado, she moved first to Germany and then to Moscow, where she lived from 1933 to 1938 while studying medicine. She married a German biophysicist, Hans-Gerhardt Fischer, and they had a daughter, Joan. Regina became a paediatrician and spoke six languages fluently, which was not surprising in view of her background. The family wanted to move back to the United States in 1939, but Hans-Gerhardt, who entertained communist sympathies, was stopped by US immigration. He moved instead to Chile. Regina and Joan however entered the United States, keeping in contact with Hans-Gerhardt by letter. In 1942, Regina had an affair with Paul Nemenyi, a Hungarian-Jewish mathematician who was involved in the Manhattan Project – the development of the atom bomb. The American grandmaster Pal Benkö told me this shocking news on a terrace on the waterfront in Willemstad, Curaçao in November 2002. 'Top secret,' he added, and I looked behind me. A week later the *Philadelphia Inquirer* made it universally known.

The FBI was interested in Regina as early as 1942. She apparently did not just work for – among others – the Army Air Force in South Dakota; her babysitter at the time also found pro-communist letters from Chile. As a good citizen and in accordance with spirit of that age, the babysitter passed these letters on to the FBI. On 9 March 1943 the birth of a certain Bobby Fischer is entered at the registry in Chicago, but Nemenyi is his biological father. His son Peter Nemenyi confirmed this when Paul Nemenyi died in 1952. Nemenyi paid monthly child support for Bobby.

Bobby Fischer is therefore 100 per cent Jewish, with a Jewish mother and a Jewish father. Joan and her half-brother Bobby, her junior by five years, were brought up by their mother. They travelled a lot in that childhood period, from Oregon to Arizona to California, and finally descended in Brooklyn. 'They made it hard for her to keep a job,' her son-in-law would later say. Regina supported herself and her children by teaching and by working in a hospital in Brooklyn. The last report from the 750-page FBI file dates from 1973 and deals with Regina's protests against the war in Vietnam.

To what extent can a person be made paranoid if he is spied upon for a long enough period of time – if your mail has already been read before you get it, if your phone has a strange buzzing sound, if casual meetings take place with people who want to know something, if your neighbours talk about you? Bobby is very sensitive and he must have felt, maybe consciously but certainly subconsciously, that something was amiss.

The final conclusion of the FBI is: Regina is not a spy, but she was a leftist activist; Bobby is not a spy either, on the contrary he dislikes Russia, while the relationship between mother and son is a bad one. In FBI file 100–102290, from 1957, there is a typical analysis that comes straight out of the world of espionage and counterespionage: it suspects that the mother is trying to draw her son into the alleged web of espionage. Bobby is then absolved as follows: 'It looks as if the subject of investigation cannot get along with her son, Bobby, and it appears that he goes against everything she wants him to do.' Case closed.

A couple of quotes from the *Philadelphia Inquirer* of 17 November 2002:

> The FBI worried that the Russians had tried to recruit the young chess prodigy on a trip he made to Moscow in 1958. FBI agents checked birth records, posed as student journalists, and considered cultivating other chess players. They hounded Fischer's mother, reading her mail, quizzing her neighbors, studying her canceled checks. They eventually decided Regina Fischer was no spy, and that the Soviets hadn't tried to enlist her son.

The FBI was particularly interested in the chess trip of Bobby Fischer to Russia in 1958.

Despite playing well in Moscow, Fischer was peeved at not being matched with the Soviets' best.

The FBI heard from another informant: Fischer had called his mother in the United States and told her, 'It's no good here.'

> '[I]t is possible that the Soviets may have made an approach to Robert Fischer to which the youth took exception,' Hoover's office wrote to the New York field office in September 1958. [They later rejected this theory.]

Fischer never had a father figure when he was growing up, and that lack was a big one. Tim Krabbé wrote in his weekly column in *AD-magazine* in March 2003:

> In 1959 when Tal won the Candidate tournament and treated the other participants, among them the 16-year-old Bobby Fischer, to a celebration dinner, his trainer Koblenz pronounced a toast. Thinking of how happy Tal's deceased father would have been, he shouted: 'To our fathers!' The remark was innocent enough, 'but,' writes Koblenz, 'you should have seen Fischer's reaction! His eyes filled with tears, and he left at once.' 'Children who miss a parent become wolves,' Fischer said later.

Fischer's Youth

While Regina worked during the day, Joan and Bobby played together. From the moment in 1949 that a chess set was unpacked, Bobby was fascinated. As Fischer wrote in his 1958 book, *Games of Chess*: 'She [Regina] often bought games at the candy store and by chance she once bought a chess game. We figured out the rules ourselves with the enclosed manual.' In the beginning they played with each other, but Joan quickly wasn't a match any more. Bobby played, like all chess prodigies in childhood, against himself. 'I would make the white moves and the black moves, played through the whole game and I would eventually checkmate the other guy,' as he later said in a Yugoslav TV interview. Regina understood that her son was intrigued by the game, and when he was seven years old she put a request in the local newspaper, *The Brooklyn Eagle,* to find opponents: 'My Son, The Chess Miracle'. It was a striking example of her commitment and intelligence. Bobby was invited to take part in a simultaneous display. He lost in the end and started to cry, because he did not know how to lose. His performance was spotted, however, and he received an invitation from the chess club of Brooklyn. He then came under the wings of its president, Carmine Negro, who became his first teacher. 'As of that moment I seriously started playing chess.' The best chess magazine in those days was the Russian *Schachmatij Bulletin*, in which the very best players analyzed their games. If you got the magazine in the post, you had to cut the pages open yourself with a knife. Bobby continued to learn from every magazine. But he had another chess school, the Hawthorne Chess Club – though it wasn't actually a club. It was the house of John Collins, a chess aficionado. Frank Brady describes in his standard work *Profile of a Prodigy: The Life and Games of Bobby Fischer* (1965) that important school of life where one's character also is formed:

> John W Collins, who contributed at least as much to the early development of Bobby as Carmine Negro, became from that time his friend, his colleague and his advisor. Collins held open house two or three times a week in Flatbush, and Bobby ate there almost as often as in his own house. Jack Collins, who was spastic and had to stay in a wheelchair all his life, was the 1952 champion of New York. He had always lived with his sister Ethel, a registered nurse. Both are gentle, kind people with a deep sense of loyalty and affection for Bobby. It is fortunate, and telling, that Bobby chose the Collins's house as his second home, which demonstrates a side of his personality he seldom

> shows to the public: that of a genial and sympathetic member of home life with a need for lasting and meaningful relationships.

Bobby played with all visitors to the Hawthorne Chess Club. He learned from the experience of the stronger players, and from the amateurs he learned the chess culture. Bobby drank it all in, and used Collins's large library extensively. He always kept that hunger for information during his active career. Fischer – unlike the rest of the world's top players – studied the games of the junior and women's championships too, because he never knew where he might find the next good idea.

Teenage Years

Bobby Fischer became champion of the United States at age 14.

A simple sentence, 11 words in all. The historical significance, the greatness behind it, causes your nervous system to tingle as you write it. You shudder with admiration. In that event, Fischer kept the seasoned 46-year-old world-class player Samuel Reshevsky at bay, among others. Fischer acquired the grandmaster title at age 15, at the time a phenomenal world record that would stand for 30 years, and only be broken in the computer age by Judit Polgar. Grandmasters nowadays get younger all the time, as the world's top players generally get younger. The average age of a top player in 1960 was 40, but in 2003 the barrier lies under 30, and world champion at the time of writing, the Ukrainian Ruslan Ponomariov, only counts 20 winters. But we live now in the era of fast knockout chess events with shorter time-limits. Times change, and you should not compare them.

A lot happens in the difficult puberty of Bobby Fischer. His mother could not handle him any more, and asked for help from social workers. She describes him as 'uncontrolled, incapable of getting along with others, without friends of his own age, and without interest in anything but chess'. A fitting description which, with a slight amendment, could apply to a lot of eccentric characters. Jan Hein Donner, the late eccentric Dutch grandmaster and writer, also considered Bobby maladjusted (*Elseviers Weekly*, 1958).

> Bobby Fischer is clearly a grandmaster. His fanaticism is without boundaries. He is really obsessed by the game of chess. Already now, at age 15, he possesses a mature, balanced style! Great possibilities for development are unlikely. He might become less nervous – the way he bites his nails during games is really spooky – and that will

make him even harder to beat, but he won't make a world champion in my opinion. As a human being too he has a lot to learn. He makes a system out of moving a piece during a game, and the moment his opponent sits up, taking the move back. He then makes the same move a moment later. This is very unusual and very annoying for the opponent. Well, Bobby Fischer is 15 years old.

Fischer already taught at a young age. He gave four tips in the magazine *Boys Life* about playing chess well: 1. Concentrate; 2. Think ahead; 3. Learn from losing; 4. Study.

In 1958, Fischer again became American champion. That gives him enough confidence to quit school and dedicate himself full-time to what really interested him: playing chess. Regina helped him look for sponsors. Bobby got airline tickets from the TV programme *I Have A Secret* to enable him to attend a chess tournament in Russia. His sister Joan went with him. Bobby played a lot of blitz games in the famous Central Chess Club of Moscow. Vasiukov asked Bobby 14 years later: 'Do you remember that you played as a boy in our club? I was there.' Bobby: 'Yes, of course I remember that.' Vasiukov: 'But do you remember the result?' Bobby: 'Why only the result? I remember the games. We played among others the French Defence.' His chess memory was phenomenal.

In 1958, Regina and Bobby went together to the offices of the United States Chess Federation (USCF), where Regina talks and Bobby is just standing there 'as if he does not belong there' (Brady). Even if Bobby did not say much, his deeds and actions did not leave the slightest doubt about his intentions. Fischer refused to represent the United States in 1958 in the prestigious chess Olympics because Reshevsky was placed on board one. That behaviour would be characteristic for his entire life. When Fischer thinks he is right, no compromises are possible – even if the consequences inflict the most harm on himself. The examples of this behaviour became increasingly grotesque during the course of his career, including walking away during the most important match of his life, the one for the world title in 1972. It has to be said in defence of Fischer that his position always contained a kernel of reasonability, although he made a mountain out of a molehill.

The Marshall Chess Club held an extraordinary meeting, especially for the 16-year-old club member Bobby Fischer. He was of course the best and only hope to catch those cursed Russians, but the club members got annoyed with his behaviour. And it is the rich club members he would need in order to start on the road to the highest peak. They wanted the best for

Bobby. Eye-witness Kaufman says in the *Philadelphia Inquirer* of February 2003:'Some of what he did was so outrageous it was decided maybe he had emotional problems.' Someone proposed a psychiatrist. Another wanted to involve the help of a prominent chess player, the endgame specialist Reuben Fine. Yet another asked aloud whether all that well-meant assistance would not be at the expense of Bobby's tremendous drive to win. The bizarre meeting ended without result. 'No one,' tells Kaufman, 'wanted to tamper with that finely tuned brain.'

In 1962 the relationship between Regina and Bobby had deteriorated so badly that they could not live together any more. Regina wanted the best for her child, and in her eyes that meant having other friends, a solid education and a regular job. That was all nonsense to Bobby. Regina left and Bobby kept the apartment in Brooklyn. Regina remarried and applied her medical knowledge to charity work like the American Reservations for Native Americans and emergency assistance in Nicaragua. Mother and son reconciled towards the end of her life (1997). Around 1990, when Bobby was a regular guest of the Polgar family in Hungary, he regularly called Regina.

The Interrupted Road to the World Title

The world's chess elite was impressed by Bobby Fischer. Tal had already expressed his admiration when Bobby was 16. His pure style of play, his hunger for truth, his will to win, never an easy draw allowing his opponent to catch his breath – never even an easy move. A well-known anecdote: Fischer played in 1959 against the old Hungarian master Barcza; he did not have an advantage but tries hard for more than 100 moves, in three separate sessions. When the game was finally drawn anyway due to lack of material, Fischer asked his opponent immediately after the game: 'Let's take another look at the game, I feel that I missed something.'

Although Fischer was then already world famous among chess players, he still could not earn a dry crust of bread from the game of chess. Occasionally a few hundred dollars for a first prize, but no more.

In 1960, Fischer played the stars from the sky on first board at the Olympiad in Leipzig. World champion Tal just managed to draw in their game. Fischer asked Tal during the closing dinner if he could read his palm. The atmosphere was good. Fischer predicts:'I see from the lines of your hand that you are a very good player, probably a world champion; but wait, I also see that you are going to lose that title to a young American.' Without missing a beat, Tal congratulated not Fischer but William Lombardy, another member of the American team.

Bobby Fischer had his own sense of humour. When the American women's champion paid him a big compliment – 'Fischer is a genius, the best player of all times'– he reacted with: 'That is true, but you cannot judge on that'; perhaps correct, but without any sense of decorum. Bobby analyzed without hidden motives, disregarding who the other person happens to be; that is a good basis to work from if you are a stand-up comedian. When the Yugoslav commentator Bjelica asked Fischer what he thought of his first meeting with Mikhail Botvinnik, the great champion of 1950 through 1963, he said: 'He is an old man.' Another time, his answer to the same question was: 'He does not have a shadow of a chance against me. Botvinnik may be world champion, but he is no Bobby Fischer.' In reply to a question in the popular *Bob Hope Show* what he thought of his opponents, he answered: 'I feel great when my opponents are in agony.' And about journalists: 'I am not afraid of anyone except for journalists.' And about whether he was the best player of all time? 'I'd rather not say that in black and white, because that sounds so conceited, but the answer to your question is: yes.' On the profound question 'What does Bobby Fischer mean to you,' he came up with: 'That is my name.' And he did not think much of all the travelling around the world. 'Why don't we build somewhere on this world a chess city, then we can keep on playing all year around.'

From 1960 onwards, Fischer gained in strength, and he appeared to be heading straight for the highest throne. He wins the interzonal tournament in Stockholm in 1962 without losing a game.

Fischer should have been happy, but he was very discontented. 'I played for six weeks, I won and I received $750. That is what I normally get for a simultaneous display.'

The last step to determine who would become the challenger to world champion Botvinnik was the candidate tournament on Curaçao in 1962. A remarkably strong field was assembled: Petrosian, Tal, Keres, Korchnoi, Geller, Fischer, Benkö and Filip. The last two had little chance. The opinions about the chances of Fischer were divided. It later turned out that Petrosian, Keres and Geller had made an agreement to draw in their games against each other, and so save energy for their games against the rest (see the interview with Korchnoi). This kind of pragmatism went against the sporting grain of Fischer, the maximalist. He thought that all of the Russians were part of this conspiracy and was enraged. 'They played like one block against me; I will never again play in one of these tournaments.' The World Chess Federation (universally known by its French acronym, FIDE, standing for Fédération Internationale des Échecs) amended the system for the World Championship cycles as a result of that outburst by Fischer.

The year 1962, and those who were present then, whether as demo board boy or assistant tournament director, are still subjects of discussion on Curaçao; their experiences are a matter of pride and competition. Even the players themselves have not completely dealt with all the emotions it generated, as became apparent in the scenes filmed for *The Wandering King* at the opening of the tournament on Curaçao in 2002. The invited players Korchnoi, Benkö and Averbakh (then the Russian trainer) used the moment they were introduced on the podium to settle a few affairs of 40 years before. They discussed an adjourned game between Benkö and Keres, an argument between Fischer and Benkö that could be heard in the corridor (see the interview with Benkö), and a few pending private affairs. The hall held its breath while listening, because they had never experienced such a heated opening ceremony. It turned out that Korchnoi had not been party to the plot devised by Petrosian. Tal had been excluded too, because he was already quite ill prior to the tournament. Petrosian won in Curaçao and went on to become the next world champion.

In an interview in *Sports Illustrated,* Fischer accused the Russians of forming a bloc: all Russian players would play into hands of their compatriot at the top of the table, he asserted, by losing their games to him. That had certainly happened in the past, and some people even say that the KGB became involved in these plots, but it seems with hindsight that is not the way things worked in Curaçao. Drawing a game and thus losing half a point was completely acceptable.

Unbending as he was, Fischer felt robbed. He began asking for higher starting fees, and when organizers tried to negotiate with him (rather than simply agreeing at once), he would not answer mail or calls. He played little between 1963 and 1966. *The Atlantic Monthly* wrote about this in December 2002: 'Even if he played little, he continued to study chess intensively. But late at night, remembers Arnold Denker, Fischer began putting flyers under car windscreens in parking lots about the supremacy of the white race. He studied anti-Semitic classics like *Mein Kampf* and *The Protocols of the Elders of Zion.*'

But when he played chess, the chess world held its breath. In 1963, Fischer won the US Championship with a maximum score of 11 from 11 (2. Evans 7.5). 'This is the way you play chess,' he let his competitors know. He was in line to participate in the next World Championship cycle, but played instead a lucrative simultaneous display tour (billed under the title

Legend on the Road). That was his answer to the low prize money on offer at the World Championship, for which he held FIDE responsible. Of course Fischer did this for himself, as this injustice was being done to him, but when the prize funds indeed started to rise, all the top players benefited. He considered FIDE to be under the direct influence of the strong Russian chess federation. That reproach too was an accurate analysis of the generally accepted situation. Even in private tournaments, the Russian grandmaster who had been contracted to come was not always the one who actually descended from the plane. The Russians, after all, reigned supreme among chess-playing nations, and they obtained quite a few debatable privileges as a result. But anyhow, Fischer could not become world champion in 1966 because he did not want to participate. Even if Petrosian extended his world title to 1969, Robert James Fischer was judged inside and outside chess lobbies as the strongest chess player of the time.

In a 1964 issue of *The Chess Correspondent* (as noted in John Donaldson's 1994 book *A Legend on the Road: Bobby Fischer's 1964 Simul Tour*, Seattle: International Chess Enterprises) there is a report by a Dr Graba, who played host to Fischer during that simultaneous display tour. 'We enjoyed his visit and I hope that Robert did so too. We were left with the impression that he is a remarkably attentive and intelligent young man. He is silently, but deeply religious; he carries the Bible with him and reads regularly in it.'

In 1965 something happened once more that easily could be interpreted as a conspiracy theory by a paranoid mind. Fischer was invited to the traditional Capablanca memorial tournament in Cuba. The previous year, Grandmaster Larry Evans had participated without any problem, and the year afterwards the American team also participated without any difficulties in the Olympiad in Havana. But Fischer did not get a visa in 1965. He consequently played by telex from America while other participants were sitting in the tournament hall. The final standings were: 1. Smyslov 15.5; 2. Fischer 15. The media of course jumped onto these bizarre circumstances. Fischer continued to amaze and public interest in the game of chess rose.

Fischer's book *Games of Chess,* with particularly objective analyses of his successes in 1957 and 1958, had already appeared by then, but the time was ripe for a new book, and that became *Bobby Fischer Teaches Chess.* 'An absolute bestseller which was printed for the first time in 1966 and of which in the end more than a million copies crossed the bookshop counters. The book would be reprinted eight times in 1972. Bobby had been working on this since 1962; he wanted to produce a book in which there were no chess technical errors.'

He fortunately played a lot in the period 1966-68, and his performance is always impressive.

- Championship of the United States 1967: 1. Fischer 9.5 from 11
- Monte Carlo 1967: 1. Fischer 7 from 9
- Skopje 1967: 1. Fischer 13.5 from 17
- Olympiad 1967: board 1. Fischer 15 from 17
- Nethanya 1968: 1. Fischer 11.5 from 13
- Vinkovci 1968: 1. Fischer 11 from 13.

Yet he still would not obtain his title in the cycle for 1969. In the candidate tournament of 1967 in Sousse, Fischer had a problem with the organization after 10 rounds. He was leading convincingly with 8.5 from 10. The problem concerned finishing an adjourned game on a Saturday. And Fischer again did not allow for a compromise. He withdrew! The heavy disappointment of that piece of bad news still weighs heavily with chess lovers. He lived for this chance, he persevered through all his problems for this. Didn't he want to be world champion? His worst opponent was Fischer himself. Boris Spassky would become the challenger in the end.

In 1969 Fischer's book *My 60 Memorable Games* was published. It is a masterpiece, translated into all languages that are spoken in the member countries of FIDE (more than 125). In most chess books there are mistakes galore, but with Fischer the trick was trying to find a small error, an improvement, an alternative. More mistakes just weren't an option.

Finally on the Right Track

The always captivating chess confrontation between Russia and the rest of the world was next played out in Belgrade in 1970. Russia had Spassky on board 1 and Petrosian on board 2. The Dane Bent Larsen wanted to be first board for the rest of the world in view of his impressive tournament results. Nobody expected that Fischer would agree to this, as he was the best player and considered himself for a long time already the best player. Fischer astonished the chess world by agreeing without a problem. He defeated the invincible Petrosian 3–1.

The World Championship cycle for 1972 started remarkably once more. Fischer had not participated in the American championship that year, and therefore was not entitled to participate in the interzonal tournament. Benkö however ceded Fischer his place (see interview with Benkö) and

Fischer then won so convincingly (3.5 points ahead) that just the tournament table in hand can provide an enjoyable evening.

Then the candidate tournament matches started, the last knockout stage. In the first stage Fischer played the strong Russian grandmaster Taimanov. That ended in 6–0. Unprecedented. Larsen, who wanted to lead 'the rest of the world', was the next to be bowled aside: again 6–0. Unheard of! Taimanov and Larsen were then finished as chess players. 'I'll crush their ego,' Fischer had once said about players who dared to challenge him. The last step was Petrosian. 'I'll feel sorry for him,' Fischer said in advance. It ended in 6.5–2.5. Incredible! (With this match and the mini-match of 1970, Fischer blows away the best defensive player of that period in a total score of 9.5–3.5.) Petrosian too was incapable of showing anything remarkable on the chess board after this defeat.

Opinion was divided in Russia about the coming match. Some people gave Spassky a small chance. They were not allowed to say that openly of course, but Fischer was extraordinarily popular among Russian chess players purely because of his style. Baturinsky, the head of the Russian chess federation and a convinced KGB man, tried to analyze Fischer's game with the help of the entire Russian chess think-tank. Everyone just analyzed as much as they could. Best-known is a report from the hand of Botvinnik. There are a few points in it that will have been of little use to Spassky (from *Russians versus Fischer*, 1994):

The opening

In unexpected positions, his choice of moves are almost always unfortunate.
Fischer does not like pawn chains. He needs the space for his pieces.

The middle game

Whenever something suddenly changes in the position (e.g. from attack to defence) then he will react without confidence.
When he loses, it is almost always in sharp positions. Technical losses are rare with Fischer.

The endgame

He likes to play Knight versus Bishop.
He prefers Bishops of opposite colours when there are Rooks on the board.

General characteristics

He is an excellent tactician and sees a lot.
When one of his pieces is attacked, he will react with a counterattack on a piece of his opponent.

A few additional observations

Do not sacrifice material against Fischer on general principles. If there is a refutation, he'll find it. Aggression by Fischer needs to be answered!

And with this wisdom, Spassky departed for Reykjavik. He did not have a chance.

1972 Fischer – Spassky

Fischer's participation in a World Championship title made this the match of the century. Would he be able to tame a whole army of the world's top players all by himself? But without its political impact this chess match would not have received the title 'Match of the Century.' Russia and the United States were waging a Cold War and the chess board was a selected battleground. There was an Iron Curtain that hermetically sealed the frontiers of the Soviet Empire. The KGB was intensively involved in the struggle, and President Nixon requested his secretary of state, Henry Kissinger, to keep Fischer on a short leash.

The match was played in Iceland, halfway between these two centres of collective and individual antagonism. If you had any kind of feeling for historical events, you would want to be there.

Fischer did not turn up at first, then came after all, and finally disappeared once more. The tension rose. According to the regulations, FIDE-president Max Euwe could have declared the match lost. Fischer got his way in everything: the quality of the chairs, the height of the table, the level of noise in the playing hall, and at the last minute, the amount of prize money, which was doubled to $250,000. That it was a very close call whether the match would be played at all raised the tension and the interest of journalists to fever pitch. Fischer had the world in his grip.

The first game was a riddle. Fischer got a Bishop-endgame in which every move, even no move, would have resulted in a draw. But he captured a poisoned pawn for no apparent reason. He was clearly not his usual self. Spassky won. Fischer refused to play the second game unless the cameras were removed. But Iceland had an agreement with filmmaker Chester Fox. There were large interests at stake. Fischer could not care less, he disappeared on a plane and lost the second game by default according to the regulations. The organizers therefore removed the cameras while gritting their teeth.

Fischer came back and apparently was reasonably content. He started to play two full points behind as if nothing had happened, but was ahead by

5–3 after eight games. Of course Fischer had a few smaller demands in between: no stiletto-heeled shoes, no children, no crackling candy paper, a few lamps to be removed, no one to sit in the first seven rows. After twelve games, halfway through the match, the Russian contingent understood that Fischer was completely superior, so they abandoned their usual secretive way of doing things. Spassky was a gentleman loser. When he unnecessarily lost game 13 after strenuously defending a mistakenly delivered check, he only shook his head. The sharp edges were now altogether removed, and it became a cosy chess party that ended in a resounding victory for Fischer.

To describe the closing party, we shall borrow a few paragraphs straight from the heart of the young Dutch journalist Böhm, who begins his story as follows:

> The weather was nice and I was 22 years old.... It was about two o'clock in the morning. I was sitting with Elisabeth in the lobby of the Hotel Loftleidir, a bit away from the bustle of the party. Things looked a bit less sharp, but I clearly thought I saw Fischer getting out of the elevator with a tennis bag in his hand. YES, HELLEWITER [for God's sake], IT WAS FISCHER!! I got up and met him just before the revolving front door: 'I am sorry to bother you but I have to tell you that you gave me enormous pleasure with your play and with your title that is now a crown on your work. I slept in toilets and risked jail but it was worth it and I want to congratulate you with the world title.' That is how it is engraved in my memory and even if the words were slightly different, that was the gist of my spontaneous speech. Fischer looked me straight into the eye and said rather seriously 'You may.' Because of the alcohol and the situation, I misunderstood his words and I thought I was only now being given a listening ear. So I repeated once more: 'Well, then I congratulate you again with your world title.' Because it was superfluous he first started laughing and because of that I did too. 'I am only a Dutchman,' and then he went through the revolving door for his nightly game of tennis with the Yugoslav grandmaster Gligoric.
>
> (from *Sic*, a Dutch literary magazine, 1991)

He was finally world champion. He had lived for it and sacrificed everything for it, and he was entitled to it. We did not grudge him it one bit.

INTERVIEWS

Viktor Korchnoi

Viktor Korchnoi was born in 1931 in Leningrad and grew up during the height of Stalin's power. Everyone in Russia was then poor, because the authorities had succeeded in enforcing total equality among its citizens. Korchnoi already knew at a young age that he wanted to be a chess player, and he is still a professional 70 years later, travelling all over the world. For this grandfatherly figure to still be one of the world's top players is itself a phenomenon. He could have been a happy man, were it not for the adversities he has had to experience, which have not allowed him peace of mind. Because of his stubbornness, there was a serious escalation of his problems with the hierarchy of the Russian chess world during the Soviet era, when it was constantly under pressure from political rulers. Korchnoi left his wife and child behind in 1976, asking for political asylum in the Netherlands. It proved to be an irreversible step with major, long-lasting consequences. Korchnoi played Karpov for the world title three times: in 1974 (because Fischer did not defend his title in 1975, this match for the right to become the challenger to the world champion became, retroactively, the final), in 1978 and 1981. Korchnoi was only allowed to smell the title each time. A lot of energy was lost in his lifelong struggle against the Russian camp (an example: when Karpov got yoghurt during a game, Korchnoi would protest that it was a kind of information transfer). Korchnoi's nickname is 'the terrible'; he quite consciously creates a tense relationship with his opponent. That gives him extra motivation and desire to win. Korchnoi can be a sympathetic person off the chess board. Granted, he is a man who wears his heart on his sleeve, but he also likes to sing a sensitive song or recite a beautiful poem when the atmosphere calls for it.

Korchnoi met Fischer as a chess player several times. One of the most memorable tournaments in which both men took part was the one in Willemstad (Curaçao) in 1962. The winner of that tournament had the right to challenge the world champion. According to Fischer, there was a Soviet plot at this tournament. The interview with Korchnoi took place on Curaçao, 40 years after the tournament in Willemstad.

What do you still remember Willemstad in 1962?

It was a memorable tournament. Many people still have memories of it. Me too, because I was one of the eight participants. It was one of the first tournaments in which I fought for the world title – without success, and I still have a bad feeling about it. But I am of the opinion that this was not only my own fault.

What exactly happened? Fischer alleged afterwards that the five Soviet participants conspired against him.

Look, he was the only one who could say anything about it. I suspected something too, but I was a Soviet citizen at the time so I could not use the press. I was not sure whether the plot was only directed against Fischer or whether it was directed against all the younger players there: Fischer, Tal and me. In retrospect, I know that Tigran Petrosian had already pulled all kind of tricks against me since 1960. That is why I am almost certain that this plot was also directed against me, just as it was against Fischer.

Fischer alleged that you too were involved in this plot, because you suddenly lost four games in a row. What was the exact story there?

The plot was like this: three Soviet players agreed to draw all their mutual games. This way they saved energy for the remaining games. The tournament was long; everyone played 28 games. It was tropically warm; I had a hard time because of the heat. It was the first time in my life that I was in such a climate. I slowly lost energy. I was leading after 14 rounds, but when the third round started, I lost four games in a row.

The three [senior players], Petrosian, Geller and Keres, had extra stamina to fight the entire tournament. And they also finished in the top of the final standings. Petrosian won, Fischer came fourth, I finished fifth, and Tal withdrew after 20 games. The plot had worked.

You could say with hindsight that the tournament at Willemstad had been arranged in a subtle manner to effect the victory of Petrosian. The head of our team, Yuri Averbakh, was his personal friend, and our coach Boleslavsky had already cooperated with him for years. Petrosian won the tournament as was required. OK, he is dead now and you should never speak ill of the dead, but he did not behave like a sportsman. Fischer was actually not only angry on his own behalf but also for me.

What does Fischer mean to you?

He has been called the best chess player of the 20th century. He had a fantastic memory, he was incredibly strong, and he beat the famous Soviet chess school all by himself. Fantastic!

After he had become world champion in 1972, he did not play a single game any more, only a couple of games on the computer. He suddenly reappeared on the scene 20 years later to play in a country which was boycotted by all right-minded people. He gave a couple of horrible interviews in which he not only accused the Russians of the plot of 1962 but of cheating during the entire century. He alleged that all matches between Karpov, Korchnoi and Kasparov had been prepared. Unbelievable. We got along well prior to that, we respected each other. But his new behaviour was the reason that all my interest in him disappeared. From that time, I don't consider him, shall we say, normal any more. When people ask me whether I now would like to play against him, I say no. I do not have any respect for him any more.

There also was something else. It became rather obvious in Montenegro that Fischer is a big anti-Semite. He was asked during a press conference: 'Are you an anti-Semite?' And he answered: 'No, I have nothing against Arabs!' It is for you to know that – well – Arabs and Jewish people both are called Semites. And this is outrageous, what he said.

They say that he is in Japan. You know, I am not curious at all how he is doing. He is not worth anything as a person as far as I am concerned. I therefore do not want to give any comment about him any more.

The chess player Fischer – as you knew him – does not exist any more?

I still want to say something about chess. In 1972 Fischer was so fantastic, he had class and he really had a lot of understanding of the game of chess. He played so incredibly badly 20 years later that it looked as if another person was sitting there. That was really remarkable.

Do you think that he ever will come back?

I have already told you that I do not want to waste another word on Bobby Fischer!

Pal Benkö

Pal Benkö was born in 1928 in France, grew up in Hungary until 1957, and then emigrated to the United States. He became a grandmaster in 1958. Although he has spoken English the larger part of his life, he still retains a heavy Hungarian accent. Benkö has taken part in the Chess Olympiad, which is played every two years, under both the American and the Hungarian flag. He has houses in both countries. Benkö is a lover of the endgame; where others start to lose concentration because the main part of the game is over, the adventure is only just starting for him. In that final phase of the game, he has created many victories out of nothing. Benkö has been crowned with many a laurel as an artist of the endgame. His creations are characterized by inventiveness. When he demonstrates one of his babies, you hardly get the chance to solve it yourself; that would take too long. He will relish in explaining all side variations and seductions while grunting 'okay?' Benkö's name will continue to live on in the Benkö Gambit, an opening in which Black sacrifices a pawn to get compensation in the long run. As he indicates himself in his book *The Benkö Gambit*, he was not the inventor of the system (it dates from the Bronstein–Lundin game of 1948), but this opening has been named after him because of his own games and his many publications in the sixties. Benkö saw Bobby Fischer grow up and was able to observe the development of that exceptional talent from very close by. They both played in the eight-player event in Willemstad in which the right to challenge Botvinnik was to be decided. Later, in 1970, it was Benkö who made the road free for Fischer by giving up his spot in the equivalent tournament, which eventually led to the world championship.

Pal Benkö, now in his seventies, is still in contact with Fischer. We talked with him during the Curaçao tournament in 2002, where he was guest of honour.

What memory of the tournament in Curaçao 40 years ago is sharpest in your mind?

It was a long and tough tournament. I think it lasted about two months. It was very tiring, but I had a very good time. I thought it a fantastic location.

Fischer alleged that the Russians conspired against him. Is that correct?

That is partially correct. Petrosian, Keres and Geller had agreed prior to the tournament to only make draws in their mutual games. And that is what also happened. They saved their energy in this way. It was a valid reason, I think [i.e. a correct analysis of the situation by Fischer], but even so I don't think he was in good form in the tournament. He would not have won the tournament anyway.

What was your relationship with him?

A very good relationship, we cooperated a lot. He often came to play blitz chess in my apartment in New York. But during the tournament [the relationship turned] a bit sour, because we got [into] some argument. But anyway we made up for it.

But there were some rumours that you had a fight in the room, because you had to share a second?

It was not a real fight. It was a little bit exaggerated, but anyway ...

What was it then? What happened?

Ah well. Let's say that we did not talk any more during the tournament. It was an unpleasant moment, but we have forgotten about it.

He later became world champion, thanks to you.

It was like this: Fischer did not play in the American championship because of some quarrel. That automatically meant that he could not play in the interzonal tournament in Palma de Mallorca. The winner of that tournament had the possibility through all kinds of matches to challenge the world champion in the end. I ceded my place to him because I thought that he had a better chance. That turned out to be correct. He won in Mallorca and after that beat Taimanov, Larsen and Petrosian and finally had the right to play against Spassky.

Thanks to you he became world champion.

Well, especially thanks to his good play.

What kind of player was he?

He was very strong. He was without doubt the best. It was very tough to play against him because he was always going for a win. He always put tremendous pressure on you.

Do you still have contact?

Yes, we occasionally call. He lived for a while in Hungary and I often met him then. You should know that I live both in Budapest and the United States.

Was he living at your address?

No, he lived in hotels. He would move to another hotel from time to time. He moved around Budapest for about six years. He then stayed for a while in Germany and then, as far [as] I know, he is in Japan. He is now living there in my opinion.

You still have contact, also in Japan?

Right, right, by e-mail and by phone.

How is he doing?

He is fine, I think. There is a rumour – he did not confirm it – that he is married and that he has a child now.

So that is the latest news?

Yes, that is the latest news about him. He is doing well, but he says he is coming back soon. I do not know when, but he is moving back again to Europe, to Hungary.

When he lived in Budapest, some of his stuff in Pasadena disappeared. What do you know about that?

He stored stuff in several places in the United States, including Pasadena. He paid for it. He showed me the cheques himself which he sent to a friend. That guy would pay the bills for the storage. But another company took over the storage space and that intermediary was too late with the payment. All his stuff was then auctioned. Bobby was completely enraged.

People in the USA say that they bought back most of the stuff and that they sent it all to Fischer in Hungary.

That is not correct. I do not think that Bobby got much back. A few people perhaps offered it for sale to him, but he did not take them up on the offer. No, he is so angry because he lost all of it. He blamed everybody: the Jews, the American government. That is of course his business. That is politics; it has nothing to do with me. He gave a radio interview in Budapest in which he vented his anger and accusations to the outside world. I arranged the interview but I told those people in advance: 'Bobby is going to say terrible things, so leave me out of it.'

The things he says are scandalous!
Of course, but what can I do about it?

Maybe ask him not to say those kind of things?
I often talked to him. But he does not change. It even got worse after he left Hungary.

Will he come back as a chess player?
Not as a chess player, unless he gets a very good offer. On the other hand, he rejected many good offers. He actually now only wants to play Fischer Random Chess. He wants to get away from all those analyses and prepared positions. I think that that is a good idea. I also worked hard on that idea, even before he did. Certainly because of the use of computers, everything depends much more on memory and not on understanding of the game any more. That is different in Random Chess.

If we want to get into contact with him, how are we going to do that?
You can send him an e-mail, but he usually does not answer.

Why not?
No idea; he does not go to chess tournaments either. He is very introverted. Even in Hungary, he did not go to chess tournaments. I played in the Bundesliga in Germany. He would then travel with me, but stay behind in the hotel. He never went to the chess hall.

What does he do all day?
I can only talk about the time in Budapest, but what it comes down to is that he gets out of bed very late, always in the afternoon. Then he'll go and eat something and at night he analyzes chess games.

Can you talk to him on our behalf? We would like to interview him.
[*laughs*] I do not know if that is of any use. I can put it up to him, but I don't know if it will lead to anything. He's the one to decide that!

Hans Ree

Hans Ree (born 1944) became Dutch champion in 1967, 1969, 1971 and 1982. He also gained remarkable results on the international stage, such as in Vancouver in 1971 where he finished joint first with world champion Boris Spassky, scoring 9 out of 11 in a field of 156 players. He only obtained the grandmaster title in 1980, however, and then belonged to a select group of 250 grandmasters across the world. Ree played against eight world champions, from Euwe to Karpov. He completed his studies as a mathematician, but he did not fancy a life of daily routine. He became a chess player instead, but did not forget to ask himself the logical question of whether it is really worthwhile to dedicate one's entire life to chess. The answer to this essential question depended always on the result of the last game. That dilemma became the inspiration for many articles he wrote. Ree wrote weekly columns in *De Haagsche Post* (from 1971 to 1983) and after that in *NRC Handelsblad* (from 1983 to the present). He has published in all some 1,500 articles in which – with reason and love, with reserve and dedication – the developments of the chess world are recorded. Even non-chess players read the remarks he makes in between the moves when analyzing; you cannot get a finer compliment as a reporter. About every three years a chess book appears from his hand, in which his trademark understated style is applied to every topic, including even his own journalism. It takes a master to catch a master – and in 2001, Hans Ree received the Max Euwe Ring. This ring, representing the Dutch chess world's appreciation of work performed for the benefit of chess in the Netherlands, is bestowed once every five years (previous recipients include Euwe, Bouwmeester, Timman and Böhm).

The interview with Hans Ree took place in the Max Euwe Centre.

You are the only Dutchman still alive who ever played against Bobby Fischer!

Yes, that is correct, Donner and Euwe are dead and the other Dutchmen did not play him.

What is that like: playing against Fischer?

Well, what is that like? I lost very quickly against him; it was during a tournament in Nethanya, Israel, in 1968. Fischer had white and introduced an opening novelty. I immediately replied with a move and then lost very rapidly. You already had the idea – even if he was not world champion then – that you were playing against a myth. That does not really help you to keep a cool head.

Why did Fischer already have the status of a myth?

Because on the one hand he was considered to be the strongest, and on the other hand because of his capricious behaviour. Fischer had played the previous year in the so-called interzonal tournament in Tunisia. He was already so far ahead halfway in the tournament that he was certain of winning it. But he withdrew because of a conflict; it had to do with playing on a Saturday. That meant that Fischer could not contest the world title in the following three years. It was a combination of enormous power and curious behaviour that made him into a myth.

What was his power?

His great versatility. As regards his openings, he was a dedicated student. He read all the Russian magazines, and [their players] were the 'crème de la crème' in those days. He was very good too in the middle and the endgame, but what he really excelled in was the clear line. His games were always lucid, never non-transparent. That was very educational for everyone. When you analyzed Fischer's games, you had the idea: yes, that is how it should be in this position.

Did you have contact with him in Israel?

Yes, quite a bit. We were about the same age. Most participants of the tournament were Israelis. Foreigners naturally draw towards each other. We walked a lot at night and we were invited afterwards by the Israeli [player] Bernstein, who lived in a kibbutz. And yes, what do you then do there: you play chess.

That is really amazing: the anti-Semite Fischer in a kibbutz.

It was already said then that he had made anti-Semitic remarks. I asked him. He said that it was indeed true, but that he had realized that this had been stupid. 'Moreover,' he said, 'I am half-Jewish.' So at that moment he wasn't, but later he was it again.

Did you follow this later on, his anti-Semitism?

Well, yes, everyone is aware of that. For instance, in the last few years he gave a number of radio interviews to a Filipino radio station. These overflow with anti-Semitic tirades.

What happened to him?

Really, I do not want to speak as a psychiatrist, but one is inclined to do so. It is in my opinion an ailment, a paranoid mental derangement that expresses itself in this manner. I do not want to say that all anti-Semites are insane, but he is that to a certain extent. He said, for instance, that the Jews want to eradicate the African elephant because their trunks make them think of uncircumcised penises. That is so bizarre that the average anti-Semite would not easily think of that.

Wasn't that meant to be a joke?

Not at all. The presenter had to laugh about it, but for Fischer it was a serious matter.

Did you have any contact with him after 1968?

No, I only met him once more during the Chess Olympics in Siegen, Germany. We exchanged friendly greetings. We were too busy with our own games. So there was no real contact.

After he had become world champion, Fischer disappeared into anonymity in Pasadena. Did chess players know anything of this situation?

To a certain extent. There were some people who said something about it, but there wasn't a great deal of publicity because Fischer instructed all his friends very firmly not to talk to journalists. Anyone who did that anyway, however innocently, was immediately out of favour and he would not see much of them any more. So you would occasionally hear something, but only minute crumbs of information.

What did Fischer bring about? At least that chess was being played for a lot of money.

It wasn't that much, really. You would be talking, in 1972, about a few hundred thousand dollars. That was of course a lot of money then, but that is very little right now. He never laid his hands on the big money until 1992. He was going to play against Karpov in 1975, for instance. Because of the myth of Fischer, suddenly $5 million was available, but the match did not take place. He could have earned a lot of money too with, say, an advertising campaign for Pepsi. But he said: 'Pepsi is bad for your teeth, I am not going to do that.' So the big money that was generated by him, he never saw any of it himself until 1992, when that strange match in Yugoslavia came about. But he started a change [in perception] in that regard. Interest in chess increased, especially in the United States. The membership of the federation multiplied, I think. That slowly trickled away again later.

Were you disappointed that Fischer did not defend his title against Karpov in 1975?

That was of course very sad. It would have been a very interesting match. Karpov was not so strong then, but despite his youth he already was a great chess player. He beat everyone convincingly. He would have been a worthy challenger for Fischer, although I think that Fischer would have won. But certainly not easily.

Fischer made a lot of demands. FIDE met him on these to a large extent. But he did not get his way on one point and so the match did not take place. Through Fischer's fault, I am inclined to say.

Were these unreasonable demands?

Yes, I thought so. Look, what he wanted was for the match to be played for ten won games, so not like previously over 24 games. You had to win ten games, then you were champion. That in itself was already a difficult question, because the organizers of such an event would not then know how long the match was going to last. You would get trouble with hiring of the playing hall and so on. You do not know how expensive it will be. They still agreed to it, but there was an extra demand.... Previously the rule was that the challenger had to win in order to become world champion. If the score was even, the title holder remained world champion. In such a match over ten won games, an even score does not occur. Fischer still wanted the advantage for the world champion retained. He wanted to remain world champion at 9–9. That meant in practice that the challenger had to win by 10–8. They thought that this demand was too severe. It was rejected, understandably.

Do you think that he still plays chess?

He is busy at the moment in promoting another kind of chess: Fischer Random Chess. The initial positions of the pieces are determined by drawing of lots. That means that you avoid all kinds of rehearsed opening theories. He probably still follows traditional chess closely. He has always stated that games between the Soviet and later Russian players were put-up jobs from both sides. He had technical chess arguments for this charge which aren't convincing in my opinion, but it demonstrated that he was still following the game.

Is Fischer then definitely lost for chess?

Well, yes, though you could imagine that he perhaps one day will play a beautiful match of Fischer Random Chess against one of today's strong players.

Against Kasparov?

Well, I don't think so. Kasparov won't feel like playing him. That is understandable. He says: I am a chess player. Random Chess is something for birthday parties.

Which of the two is the best player?

Let's see, chess has changed and progressed. The knowledge of today is unbelievably more extensive than in the past. That is because of computers, databases and the fast dissemination of information. Today's knowledge is more extensive, so Kasparov is the better player. But if you ask: who is – as regards talent and chess power – the greatest, then I would, after brooding and hesitating for a long time, still choose Fischer.

Harry Sneider

Harry Sneider (born 1941) is a special friend of Bobby Fischer. He doesn't play chess, but is a world champion weight-lifter, with a record for his current age group of 230kg. He has a sports school in California in which he gives fitness training. Sneider and Fischer met in 1972 at the University of Pasadena, where Fischer gave a lecture about the life of a chess player. That was at the invitation of Herbert W Armstrong, the major figure behind the Worldwide Church of God, whose headquarters are located in Pasadena. Fischer was already a member of that Christian fellowship before he came to live there in the late 1960s. On a tour of the campus Fischer went to the fitness centre where Sneider was teaching. They started to talk and Sneider spoke about his coaching of great American champions, like high-jumper Dwight Stones and racing-car driver Danny Sullivan. Fischer was impressed, and since he, in contrast to most top chess players of that day, considered physical education important, he asked if Sneider would like to train him. 'I want to have arms just like you,' Fischer said that first time. Their friendship grew from then on, even though their personalities were quite different. They learned from each other and talked about everything. Sneider was also a member of the Worldwide Church of God, so their cooperation got the blessing of Herbert W Armstrong. A subject they never discussed was chess. That is most probably one of the pillars of their friendship, which lasts until today.

In an interview at his sports school in California, Sneider tells us what Fischer's life looked like in the period that he was invisible for the rest of the world.

Please tell us something about your relationship with Bobby Fischer.

Bobby and I got along very well with each other. He trusted me as a friend. Our personalities were quite different, but I could fulfil his needs – namely, he wanted to be physically fit so he could play chess well. He was able to focus very well on one thing, but you also need discipline, and that is what coaches are for. That is my profession. I do not play chess, and that is also the reason that our friendship is so good. We never discuss it. We talk about all kinds of other things, like fitness, life, music and the Bible. I studied theology, and Bobby was very interested in that. He had an unbelievable hunger for information. He read something like 25 magazines in a weekend. I saw him read once while he listened to five radios at the same time. Fascinating.

How was his physical condition?

When Bobby came back from Reykjavik he was in top form. There was a policeman in Iceland, Sammy, who engaged in combat sport. He trained there together with Bobby. Fischer had trained prior to that for months, because he really believed in a good preparation. He loved power-training with weights, he swam 45 minutes a day and he was a 'world champion' walker. His mother also did that very well. He takes enormous strides, and can keep that up for three and a half hours. He also liked playing tennis and he watched his food very closely. He drank pints of carrot juice and ate a lot of salads. He took a sauna every day and had a massage. That was his daily routine. Actually, I'm disappointed he did not maintain it.

I gained a lot from my cooperation with him. I worked as a trainer at the 1984 Olympic Games with 20 sportsmen in nine different disciplines. Fischer taught me how you can focus on one thing. He taught me what winning is. The mental aspect of winning was no problem any more, because I worked with a genius in that field. He also studied a lot. Before the match in 1972, he studied 16 hours a day. He has read 100,000 books, he has an enormous memory capacity. In world history there are people like Mozart and Einstein, but Fischer is in his way also unique. Someone like that is born once every 100 years. He is really a treasure for humanity. I hope he comes back and starts playing chess again, so we can enjoy the talent that God gave him.

Can you tell us a bit more about Bobby's youth?

He had an unusual youth. His father abandoned him at a very young age. His mother worked, which meant that Bobby was alone a lot. His sister Joan was highly talented and did her own thing. Bobby probably missed homeliness in his youth. We sometimes take for granted [what] it is to have families and how wonderful a blessing it is to have that. That is why he loved being part of our family. And he basically would like coming over very often, to have that love and friendship. My wife cooked and

Bobby felt at ease here between us and the three children. There are basically many others whom I introduced to him, and who did similar things in our church. The church adopted him as a long-lost uncle or long-lost friend. Nobody saw him as the great champion, we considered him more as someone who could use a bit of support. They (kind of) smothered him with love; maybe we got him a little soft, looking back. That does not mean I take responsibility for him not playing chess any more, but certainly it could have been better keeping him a bit on the edge, possibly. When he was hungry, that is when he became the big champion he was. The drive to perform then disappeared. He did not live as a great champion any more.

How did Fischer live in Pasadena?

Bobby had his own apartment, which had been made available through the church. He had little luxury, but it was enough. I often went there. We often ate exotic food. He loved Indian and Chinese food. There were regularly people from the press at the front door who wanted to catch a glimpse of Fischer. They would stand with their cameras and microphones at the ready and then would ask me: 'Why doesn't he come out?' It was a challenge for him to stay out of sight. He now apparently is one of the most challenging "missing persons" to spot.

Until when did he live here?

Bobby lived here quite a long time, I think from 1976 or 1977. But in the period that he was so pampered, something else happened. Dissident people, people who had different views from the church, entered into his life. They began to share so-called inside information about different personalities. This destroyed his confidence in the church. He began to criticize people within the church. He even criticized me for staying with the Worldwide Church of God. And he began to listen to other religious programming. Those people made good use of him. They interviewed him for their paper. They recorded him on tape and they used those tapes for their own purposes. He was very upset about that, and then left [Pasadena]. He started to travel inside the USA and later in Europe. He went to Germany to buy leather goods and shoes, and to Argentina, and he was often in Tokyo. He is crazy about electronic gadgets, TVs and cameras. About ten years ago I received a picture postcard from him in Germany; contact was then restored.

Something remarkable happened at that time. There was a Hungarian girl who wrote a wonderful letter to Fischer. She was wondering why he didn't play chess any more, because chess players all over the world would enjoy that. In consequence of that letter he started to train again. She saw to it that a return match against Spassky was organized in 1992 for $5 million. I came along to that island [Sveti Stefan], I cannot remember in which country [Yugoslavia]. Fischer won. He was then very close to that girl. Unfortunately, the relationship broke down.

In 1998, I went once more to Budapest. Fischer wanted me to stay there, but my family lives in the USA and I won't abandon them. That was the last time I saw him. I was asked a few times to come to Tokyo or the Philippines, but I didn't get around to it.

So you still have contact with him.

I talk with him twice a month. He is now working on his chess clock in Tokyo and on his own chess game, Fischer Random Chess. We sometimes e-mail and I occasionally send him poems as inspiration. Bobby also may call out of loneliness and we then talk for hours. He does not trust everybody. I hope that this interview does not damage our friendship.

Why do you then give this interview?

I rejected very many interviews. But this is more like a public call to Bobby. I want him to start playing chess again, he has to use his talents. Thousands of children in the entire world look up to him. He has to share his knowledge. I am therefore asking you when you hear this: 'Please Bobby, join the chess world again! I want to help you. You belong to the [Michael] Jordans and the Pelés of the world.' Normally speaking I do not do that sort of thing, but I have a good feeling about this. He is not a madman who flipped. I am sure that he can still make it very difficult for Kasparov and all those others. I would only want him to be a bit more positive about the USA. I love this country, I consider the things he sometimes shouts quite horrible.

How do you view Bobby Fischer's future?

Bobby has to do two things. He has to get Fischer Random Chess generally accepted, and he has to start training again. I hope in this way that I shall get him so far that he gets out of his shell a little more. But we must be a touch careful with him. Over five years he lost his mother, his sister and his cousin. He's had a tough time. He is very sensitive. Many people made use of him for their own purposes, and abused him. Someone from the *Los Angeles Times* once called him a holy idiot. That does something to you, don't be mistaken about it. Bobby Fischer is not perfect, but this just goes too far. He goes into hiding for that.

Part 2

After 1972
The Fischer Legend

Fischer as world champion

Bobby Fischer, the world champion of chess, who had beaten the Russians, was welcomed in his homeland as a hero. In City Hall in New York, he symbolically received the keys to the city. He told his story on the highest-rated TV shows. But the greatest honour he got is that chess fever raged all over the world, and therefore also in America: chess clubs popped up like mushrooms after a heavy autumn downpour. Everybody wanted to play chess. And everybody wanted to do business with him; he could have been a multi-millionaire. All his life he had scorned the low prize money available in the game of chess, which did not correspond to the tough work required; he had stuck to his guns on principle whenever he did not get what he felt was his due. And he had triumphed all through his own merit; the world was now at his feet. What a past! What a future!

But Fischer reacted in his own way. A million-dollar contract with Pepsi was dismissed by him with: 'I don't drink that stuff.' Also a $250,000 offer for a game of blitz chess in Las Vegas was rejected. *Esquire*, in an article published in 1992, summed up more of the offers that had been made to him 20 years before: President Marcos offered $3 million to participate in a tournament in the Philippines; the Shah of Persia $2 million; Qatar, South Africa, Chile, Argentina all put a lot of money on the table. A millionaire from Spain offered $4 million, but Fischer's reaction was: 'Nah. The amount is too low.'

Not a single offer passed his scrutiny. Fischer did not want people to swindle him, and he therefore did nothing at all.

He returned to Pasadena and was cradled in the safe arms of the Worldwide Church of God (see Harry Sneider interview, page 48). In order to be slightly more anonymous, he changed his name to Robert D James.

From *The Atlantic* in 2002: 'He lived in WCG-owned apartments, was entertained at fancy restaurants, and flew to exotic spots in the Church's private jet. And Fischer was set up on the first dates of his life, with attractive WCG members.'

Fischer was embraced as the prodigal son, but the price of this hedonistic life was high. Fischer said later, in 1977, when he had turned his back on his faith: 'They cleaned out my pockets. Now my only income is a few royalty cheques from my books. I was really very foolish.'

That Fischer wanted to catch his breath for a while after the enervating match with Spassky was clearly understood by the chess world, but the sabbatical should have been over after six months. Surely there had to be an itch to play? The power of hunger for the chessboard is like no other. But nothing happens. A full year went by. Nothing. The air in the chess world buzzed with rumours. Did Fischer consider himself too good to play against humans? Was he waiting for an invitation for an intergalactic contest?

There was a sign of life after two years. In the chess magazine *Chess Life and Review*, in November 1974, Fischer wrote a letter to his old chess friend Larry Evans who had made (in his opinion) an error of judgement. A reader had taken a chess problem from Horowitz's *All About Chess*. In the book, black lost in the next move, but the reader had suggested an alternative that seemed to hold out the promise of a draw. In the magazine, Evans had complimented the reader on the suggestion, describing it as 'a very neat resource'. Fischer wrote castigating him for endorsing the reader's suggestion (perhaps motivated by Evans being the only person at *Chess Life* who had publicly opposed the conditions Fischer was then trying to impose for the 1975 World Championship game with Karpov):

> This is typical of your disappointing inclination to provide superficial and incorrect answers. After 29.Kd3, Nxf5 30.Be5! Black still has a very long way to go in order to draw the game. Worse still, my opinion is that Black's position is hopeless.... Maybe you'll still try and demonstrate some rinky-dink draw to your readers in this endgame, but remember you're not fooling me one bit – Black is dead lost.

When Fischer started negotiation about the conditions for the world title match in 1975, the chess world thought, with relief, that it showed that he still had the urge to play. His analyses were still crystal-clear and without error, and it seemed that even if he only came down off the mountain once every three years to defend his title, people would still be content.

1975 came around. Challenger Anatoly Karpov was completely prepared, and the chess world tensely awaited the result of the negotiations. It was almost impossible to complain about the prize fund; there seemed to have been at least $5 million available. But there was no match, and Fischer lost his title, even if he was probably still the strongest player at that moment (see Karpov interview).

The chances would be different a year later. Karpov wanted to prove that he was not only world champion on a technicality. He played a lot, won everything, and grew in strength, and he continued to do so until 1985. But even though Karpov still tried to arrange an unofficial match against Fischer in 1976, it did not come to fruition in the end. KGB documents that have been released in the meantime show something of the strategy behind a potential Karpov–Fischer match. From *Russians versus Fischer* (Secret letter no. 3403c, 20 October 1976):

> The Ministry of Sport of the Soviet Union still considers it undesirable that such a match is held.... If Fischer and his agents will propose concrete conditions, we would consider it desirable to keep the negotiations going and to make counterproposals in cooperation with A Karpov that would create a favourable situation for the world champion [i.e. Karpov], and that would be unacceptable for R Fischer.

Bobby Fischer is therefore a subject of conversation at both the FBI and the KGB; he was, and remained, afraid of both organizations. That this led to both paranoid thoughts and behaviour is certainly true, but they had a basis in reality. Because he also had a strong dislike for journalists, organizers, lawyers and other 'creeps', whom he thinks are all after his money, there was not much else left than isolation.

Paranoia

In 1977, however, a booklet entitled *Bobby Fischer Heute* (Bobby Fischer Today) suddenly appeared from the pen of Yves Kraushaar. What nobody succeeded in doing, this amateur had managed to do – to meet and interview Fischer. He got a secret address through several intermediaries. But before he succeeded in getting into the same room as Fischer, he had to do quite a bit of work. He had strange telephone conversations with a personal assistant, he suddenly had to count to 33 in German, he had to make an appointment on a deserted road while a car made contact with light signals, he drove around at random in Pasadena and its surroundings. It is clear that the Church – then still protecting him – screened off its generous donor quite efficiently. The appointment finally turned out to be in a modern office building. Kraushaar: 'He received me in a very good mood. Radiant, with a firm handshake: Bobby Fischer.'

Fischer did not want anything more to do with FIDE, he said, although this organization had not had many opportunities to do wrong since 1972. Fischer still considers himself world champion; when Kraushaar addresses him as ex-world champion, he is immediately corrected.

Not long afterwards, Fischer broke off all ties with the Worldwide Church of God. It is possible that the privileges stopped when the chicken had been stripped bare of its feathers.

Fischer got on the road, staying in dingy hotels. His fine clothes lost their shine and were not replaced. In its 2002 article *The Atlantic Monthly* wrote:

> He bought great quantities of exotic herbal potions, which he carried in a suitcase, to stave off the toxins he feared might be secretly put in his food and water by Soviet agents. According to a 1985 article in *Sports Illustrated,* Fischer medicated himself with such esoteric remedies as Mexican rattlesnake pills ('good for general health') and Chinese healthy-brain pills ('good for headaches'). His suitcase also contained a large orange-juice squeezer and lots and lots of vitamins. He always kept the suitcase locked, even when he was staying with friends. 'If the Commies come to poison me, I don't want to make it easy for them,' he explained to a friend. Perhaps the most telling sign of his rapid mental deterioration was that he insisted on having all his dental fillings removed. 'If somebody took a filling out and put in an electronic device, he could influence your thinking,' Fischer confided to a friend: 'I don't want anything artificial in my head.'

Fischer was still playing chess, but his opponent was now a computer. He sent handwritten letters to the new magazine *Computer Chess,* for the attention of chief editor Penrod. Fischer wrote that he had played against a computer on which a chess program was installed, and that he was disappointed in the program's weakness. He was also very unhappy about the design: 'The lines on the chess board are numbered and the ranks are alphabetical. How is this possible?!' He describes the games he played on it. In his opinion, 'It is almost impossible to lose an endgame.' Fischer would write more on the subject later – the development of computer chess was then still in its infancy (see appendix 3: 'What is Genius?', page 38).

A book would appear in 2001 entitled *Die Handschriften großer Schachmeister* (The Handwriting of Great Chess Masters) by the Swiss Robert Bollschweiler. This graphologist analyzed, among others, Fischer's handwriting, making use of his 1977 letters. He came to the following conclusion:

> As unusual as Fischer's personality is, just as unusual is his handwriting: it does not form a whole, is independent and it lurches a lot. However, there is no chaos as one would think at first sight.... It remains a fact that the lurches are considerable and point at an unbalanced man, who is torn here and there by inner contradictions. Fischer appears to be very strongly entrapped in his own world and he clearly lacks the ability to adapt.

That all may be true, but it would have been more convincing if the analysis had been made in 1977, and without knowing whose handwriting it was. In 2001, it seems to be a case of having 20/20 vision with hindsight.

In 1981, Karpov had retained the official world title by once more stopping the challenge of Viktor Korchnoi. In that year, as Fischer was, in his own words:

> walking peacefully and lawfully towards Lake Street in Pasadena across from the Kaiser Permanente medical offices, a policeman in a car suddenly pulled up alongside the curb and said he wanted to talk to me because I fitted perfectly the description of a man who had just committed a bank robbery. I politely told him he had the wrong man and I hadn't committed a bank robbery, and that I didn't know anything about it whatsoever.

Fischer had to tell the policeman where he lived, but the situation is complicated because Fischer was lodging here and there with friends because of lack of money. He was handcuffed, taken to the police station and brutally interrogated. In his 1982 pamphlet, 'I Was Tortured in the Pasadena Jailhouse', Fischer gives the description of the officer who:

> without any provocation of any kind on my part, grabbed my throat with one hand and started choking me by the neck, pushing me backward in the chair (throughout all this 'interrogation', savagery and physical assault, I was seated and with my hands handcuffed behind my back). I am sure I could easily recognize him if I saw him again. For example I could easily pick him out of a police line-up.

According to the pamphlet, they threw Fischer, naked, into a bare police cell. Next day, he was transferred, still naked, to an isolation cell. 'My body and flesh are still in pain as I write these lines eight or ten days later,' he wrote. He was suffering from hunger and thirst. He heard the indictment two days later: 'interfering with the duties of an officer'. Fischer was released on bail. He never heard of the charge again. He finished his heart-wrenching report as follows: 'To say that the whole thing stinks and is a frame-up and set-up is to put it mildly.' The pamphlet is signed 'Robert D. James (professionally known as Robert J. Fischer or Bobby Fischer, The World Chess Champion)'.

Fischer is, without doubt, prone to conspiracy theories, but he is not the kind of man to tell an outright lie about a concrete experience: it is alien to him; it is not logical. Anti-authoritarian as he is, he can be depended on to have annoyed the average right-wing policeman in word and deed. This horrible experience cannot simply be dismissed, however, as the author of the 2002 article in the *Atlantic Monthly* seems to do.

Fischer made a living during the next few years by interviews and chess lessons, at $5,000 a shot. The interviews are sometimes about a possible comeback (see the interview with Arnfried Pagel, page 84). Grandmaster Biyiasas played some ten blitz games against Fischer in 1981 and lost all of them. Biyiasas said: 'The most depressing part is that I did not end up in an endgame from the middle game. I cannot recall a single endgame.'

It is of course difficult to estimate how strong someone is when he does not play any more. Even if Fischer remains a living legend, the top rank of active players also demands admiration at the same time. The hegemony of

Karpov was attacked in 1984 by the next historic talent, Gary Kasparov. This time not East against West, but Old Russia against New Russia. The second match of the century! They carry on with an insane, unending struggle. Victory in this match all depends on six won games, draws not counting. This formula had already been proposed by Fischer for his match in 1975. It originated from the discontent about the usual formula in which the player who is ahead can win with mere draws, counting on a limited number of games. A draw then does not mean equal sharing of a point. Fischer thought that there should be a real struggle. The disadvantages of that system, however, also became apparent in 1984. The score was 4–0 in favour of Karpov after 11 games and it could already have been over and done with by then. But the machine halted. After an interminable series of draws, the score only reached 5–0 after the 27th game. From then on, Kasparov put his faith into drawing games. Karpov could not keep that up physically and started to commit blunders. After 48 games and half a year of playing, with the score stuck at 5-3, the Filipino president of FIDE, Campomanes, intervenes. The match is declared null and void, with both players protesting, and consequently has to be replayed.

Kasparov proved that had learned his lesson in the next match in 1985, when he won and was from then on the best player. Now, in the modern history of chess, only Emanuel Lasker has been world champion for longer than Kasparov (see list of world champions, page 130).

Fischer insulted the top Russian players, past and present, by alleging that all their games were prearranged (something Petrosian, Geller and Keres had indeed been guilty of in 1962). That the KGB and even higher authorities were involved in the past in some of these developments is well known. Some results were fixed. Bronstein alleged in 1951 that he had been prevented from becoming world champion because Botvinnik had better contacts among the party elite. Taimanov was socially punished in 1971 because of his loss to Fischer; from then on, he was not allowed to travel abroad, he could not perform as a concert pianist, and all his privileges were at once withdrawn. But the new Russia makes allowance for different kinds of relationships, and today there are many top ex-Soviet players who now play from their new home countries, and for their own benefit. Fischer's insult would have been partially correct before *glasnost* in the mid-1980s; after that time his suspicions do not make sense.

Throughout the 1980s, there is another Fischer refrain that is getting louder all the time: the classical game of chess badly needs renewal! Changes to the rules had been made before in chess history, like castling and capturing 'en passant', which were introduced at the end of the 16th century. Chess was after all derived from the way war was waged around the beginning of our Christian era, and as wars have been conducted more quickly, so chess has accelerated too. In the current age of unmanned fighter aircraft that take decisions autonomously, there are more than enough reasons for yet another acceleration. Fischer states that in classical chess, even the best games by top players only start to take on a character of their own after 20 moves, because too much knowledge is available about the permutations of play in the early moves, which after all start from a known position that is always the same – the opening layout of the pieces on the board. Too many openings have been overanalyzed, so whoever has the best computer now wins. Fischer showed how to introduce something new to break up this pattern. He introduces two radical changes: Fischer Random Chess and the Fischer clock. His proposals at first trickled through into the chess world. They became more concrete in the 1990s, and slowly gained more support.

In Fischer Random Chess, the pawns remain where they usually are, on the second row, but the pieces behind them are arranged in a random manner. Nobody knows in advance what the initial position will be. The start of the game is therefore not *White begins* but *White begins to put his pieces down*. Black can choose to follow meekly or choose another set-up. This radical proposal, in which the value of opening preparation is eliminated, had already been proposed at the beginning of the 20th century, but Fischer is the first one who seriously started working on the idea. Random Chess began to surface here and there, but because classical chess has seen a revival, the Random variety appears to be dying of too many draws. This is especially so because the ever-growing use of the computer has meant that there is no real inducement to play with variable initial positions.

The Fischer clock is a digital clock that you can adjust in many different ways. For instance, lightning games of one, three or five minutes per game. The current competitive games are played according to a time limit of 40 moves in 120 minutes, then 20 moves in the third hour, and finally 15 minutes extra to finish the game. The Fischer clock does that perfectly. A variant used in tournaments is the formula of 40 moves in the first 90 minutes, in which every move will gain each player 30 seconds additional reflection time (the so-called Fischer bonus). That means that you do not have to lose on time in a won position; this is a big improvement compared with the mechanical clock. These digital clocks have been completely accepted throughout the chess world, but Fischer has not received, quite unjustly, any royalties for the idea. If Fischer had been the official world champion, his proposals for Random Chess and the clock would probably have been accepted more quickly, and his name would be more closely connected to these historic changes.

In 1988, Fischer came into contact with Petra Stadler. She told her story in *Bobby Fischer – The Way He Really Is: A Year with the Chess Genius* (*Wie er wirklich ist – Ein Jahr mit dem Schachgenie*, 1995). He was not psychologically well, and his delusions had become grimmer. Fischer talked a lot with Petra about Jewish world conspiracy theories; he frequented anti-Semitic bookshops. Hitler intrigued him; Fischer liked watching German movies about World War II.

In 1990, Fischer went to Belgium at the invitation of Bessel Kok, founder and director of Swift, an organization for international banking. Kok, a passionate chess amateur, is not only closely involved in the traditional super-tournaments promoted by Swift, but he also established together, with Jan Timman, the Grand Master Association, a trade union for professional chess players. Once in a while the GMA takes action against FIDE, sometimes even successfully, and that was to Fischer's liking (see interview with Timman, page 88).

1992 Fischer – Spassky

Fischer visited Germany after his Belgian trip and looked up Petra. He stayed for a year, often changing hotels to outsmart journalists. The chess world knew about Fischer's stay, and also of his madness. Kasparov was so far ahead of his challengers by this point that people only credited the by-then unknown power of Fischer with any chance of success against him. Who would make an attempt to get Fischer behind the chess board, now that he was living outside his by-then cursed America?

It was at this point that Boris Spassky sought contact with Fischer, putting out feelers for a potential return match. Spassky had thrown off the Soviet yoke, lived in France, and has spoken of Fischer only in praising terms. The right person, the right moment and the right location were sought. Fischer said he was prepared to play if $5 million in prize money were made available. He was apparently so fed up with his lack of financial independence that he wanted to get over the problem once and for all. He was even prepared to risk life and limb for it. When the news report started circulating, no one believed that the match would actually take place. Fischer had not played a serious game for 20 years, and although Spassky is hardly the most dangerous opponent any more – he was ranked 99 in the world in 1992 – he had at least continued to play.

Plans for the match developed during the time of the first Gulf War. It was clear on whose side Fischer was in this conflict. In 1997, Hans Ree wrote in his book *Schitterend Schaak* (Brilliant Chess):

> Fischer tried to send a telegram to Saddam in which he congratulated him for occupying Kuwait, and said that he may use the name of Fischer for propaganda purposes. As his correspondence address, he gave Petra's home address. She is getting a bit fed up with the association with Bobby.

Fischer had not seen a tournament hall for 20 years and was in the position of facing a renowned grandmaster who no longer won often, but did not lose many games either. What should he do? He might have immediately collected all his opponent's games and studied them as hard as possible in the months leading up to the tournament, and perhaps played exercise games. But not so Fischer.

Fischer was in Hungary with a new girlfriend, 19-year old Zita Rajcsanyi. According to bosom friends, it was Zita who gave Fischer the power to actually renounce his life of a hermit. In terms of his technical chess skills, there was apparently no problem, but all the other obstacles seemed to worry Fischer: press conferences, journalists, his safety, organizers, the crowds of 'creeps'. Fischer wanted to control everything. And new problems were added, because the organization of the tournament had been assigned to Yugoslavia, and that country was in the middle of a bloody civil war. The tournament's sponsor, Vasiljevic, had made a fortune as an arms dealer. The United Nations forbade anyone from doing business with a country at war. Fischer said he could not care less. A warning was issued to Fischer by the Ministry of Finance in Washington that playing in Yugoslavia was in contravention of the law, attracting a fine of $250,000, or ten years in jail, and probably both.

Yet, the match was staged, against all expectations. Whoever was the first to win ten games was to be the winner; draws didn't count. The location where the action took place was bizarre: the vacation island of Sveti Stefan, on the Adriatic coast of Montenegro, is connected with the mainland by a single road, so it can be made secure easily. At the opening ceremony on 2 September, 20 years to the day after Reykjavik, Fischer was asked what he thought of the threats made against him. Fischer ostentatiously grabbed the official message from Washington, spat on it, and tore it in pieces in front of the reporters. In the 1992 book *A Chess Genius Returns* the tournament's chief arbiter, Schmid, said: 'That was not a diplomatic master move, but it was indeed testimony of great civil courage.' From that day on, Fischer could not go back.

The match was of course played with a prototype of the Fischer clock. Fischer had White in the first game and won as if no time had passed! It was a typical Fischer game: each move was part of the large plan, the positional moves, the regrouping of pieces, the sacrifices, the finale: a masterpiece, worthy of a world champion (see the analysis of this game in appendix 3, page 145).

It is clear after five games that Fischer was still using his old repertory from 1972. He did not have anything extra up his sleeve; he had not even prepared himself against Spassky as an individual. That is abundantly clear from his last-minute request to the trade journal *New In Chess* to search for Spassky's past games. Chief editor Dirk Jan ten Geuzendam departed from Haarlem with a chess program and a print-out of about 1,500 Spassky games, and only arrived during the fifth game (see Ten Geuzendam interview, page 93). From *New In Chess* 1992:

> Fischer leads by 5–2 after 11 games and the required 10 won games have been pocketed convincingly after 30 games; the score

is then 10–5. If Fischer and Spassky had played according to the 1984 formula of Kasparov and Karpov – the first one to win six games is the winner of the event – then the match would have finished after 17 games and within six weeks. Fischer came, he raged, he won.

When you study the reports and the commentaries, some experts clearly had great difficulty in retaining their technical objectivity, perhaps because they considered Fischer's political ideas objectionable. Yet this match may have been much better than it was judged at the time. Of course Fischer occasionally blundered, but the many pieces of art that led to his victory are impressive, despite the fact that the artist had not shown anything for the previous 20 years.

Grandmaster Duncan Suttles in the British Columbia chess magazine *Counterplay* wrote in 1994: 'I believe that his strategic play is stronger than 20 years ago. There was a lot of brain-work in it. He did not sit idle and do nothing during the intervening period.'

The Aftermath

What could he do now? Fischer was 50 years old and a millionaire again, but he could not go back to the United States, where he had become *persona non grata*. He arranged for all his property in the United States to be put into storage, and asked a friend to pay the monthly rent. He stayed for a while in Yugoslavia, and was then spotted in Hungary, where he stayed for four years. He was much indebted to Zita, and the relationship lasted for about a year. Zita too wrote a book about her relationship with Fischer. Hungary has a tremendous chess culture and perhaps Fischer felt even more at home in what was, after all, the country of his biological father, Paul Nemenyi. He was a regular guest at the home of the (ironically Jewish) Polgar family in Budapest, with their three child prodigy daughters, Zsuzsa, Zsofia and Judit. Judit is the youngest and, at the time of writing, the strongest; she now stands 10th in the world rankings, and has defeated Gary Kasparov. Zsuzsa (Susan) Polgar, quoted in *The Atlantic Monthly* in 2002: '"I remember happy times in the kitchen cutting mushrooms," Susan says. "He's very normal in that sense, very pleasant."' Even if Fischer no longer played official games, he helped the Polgar sisters with their analyses. They played a lot of Fischer Random Chess. There was even talk of a match between Fischer and Judit Polgar using Fischer Random Chess. Fischer appeared to be living an almost normal life until his Jewish conspiracy theories put an end to his inspiring cooperation with the Polgars (see Zsofia Polgar interview, page 106).

Fischer still hung around in Europe a while, and then went to Japan. Japan was very congenial to Fischer: he had always liked Japanese cuisine, he liked technological novelties, there are few Jews in Japan, and few chess players.

In 1998, the bad news reached him that his storage space in Pasadena had been vacated because of non-payment, the required $480 dollars in rent not having been paid on time. It seemed that the owners wanted to do something else with the space and were looking for a reason to get rid of Fischer's belongings. Fischer was enraged. Bob Ellsworth, a friend of his from his time in the Worldwide Church of God, had been negligent. In *The Atlantic Monthly*, Ellsworth had this to say:

> 'It was my responsibility to pay the bill, and I didn't pay it because I didn't know there were new owners,' Ellsworth says. 'So they put Bobby's stuff up for auction. I felt really bad and spent about $8000 of my own money buying back all the significant memorabilia.' The storage room was not a treasure trove worth 'hundreds of millions of dollars', as Fischer has claimed. 'A lot of it,' Ellsworth says, 'was

old magazines and things that were of personal interest to Bobby: books on conspiracy theories, racy Mexican comics, lots of John Gunther books. Things you could go down to Olvera Street and replace for a dime a copy. That stuff I passed on. But anything of intrinsic value I snagged.' At the auction, Ellsworth acquired 'about 80 percent' of the various lots.

Harry Sneider corroborates Ellsworth's story, and says that his son personally delivered the reclaimed memorabilia to Fischer in Budapest. When a list of the numbered lots was read off to him, Sneider confirmed that each one is again in Fischer's possession. Lot 151: Box Lot of Telegrams to Bobby Fischer During World Chess Championship. 'Delivered.' Lot 152: Box Lot of Books Inscribed to Bobby Fischer (not by authors). 'Delivered.' Lot 153: From the People of New York given to Bobby Fischer—Leather Scrapbook with Letter and Telegram from Mayor John V Lindsay of New York City. 'Delivered.'

We can safely assume that Fischer thinks differently about this. An antiquarian series of comic books can have both emotional and large monetary value. In an interview on Filipino radio in 1999, Fischer talked about the series of Mexican comic books that Ellsworth mentioned, and he gave out Ellsworth's home address, so that anyone who understood Fischer's frustration could pay 'a visit'. Fischer saw a conspiracy theory in this too, even though Ellsworth had performed his task correctly for seven years.

Since 1999, Fischer has aired his opinion through the ether. Both Radio Calypso in Hungary and Radio Bombo in the Philippines have given Fischer airtime to do so. It is the only way that Fischer will now talk publicly: live. No editing tricks, preferably no questions either; Fischer rather talks solo about his pet subjects. When Fischer really gets going on his favourite subjects, his voice regularly rises in pitch. It is not pretty to listen to, irrespective of the language, irrespective of the message: here is someone speaking who is out of his mind (see Radio Interviews, page 117).

When Fischer told radio Bombo with reference to the tragic events of 11 September 2001: 'This is all wonderful news. It is time for the US to have their head kicked in … . What goes around, comes around,' and finished his unstable tirade with: 'I want to see the US wiped out. F**k the Jews. This is a wonderful day. Death to the USA, f**k the USA,' friend and foe alike had had as much as they could stomach. Even his last fans in the United States publicly distanced themselves from him. Fischer is not a victim of sex, drugs or rock 'n' roll, but a victim of his own mental illness.

Fischer has grown increasingly lonely. All his close relatives have died, one after another. His mother Regina Wender passed away in 1997, then not long afterwards his half-sister Joan, and in 2000 his half-brother Peter Nemenyi became incurably ill. Fischer could not attend their funerals in the United States – he would have been arrested as soon as he entered the country. So Fischer decided to start a new family. He asked his chess friend Torre to look around in the Philippines for a suitable woman to carry his baby. In early 2000, Fischer chose the 22-year-old Chinese–Filipina Justine Ong: she has nothing to do with chess, and does not have any plans to write a book about their relationship. At the end of 2000, Justine became the mother and Fischer the father of a daughter by the name of Jinky Ong. Just like his biological father, Fischer pays child support, and goes from time to time to Manila to see Jinky. What will Jinky be when she grows up? And what will happen to her father, Robert James Fischer?

INTERVIEWS

Lothar Schmid

Lothar Schmid (born 1928) was a good chess player himself, but is above all things known for his large and special collection of chess books, and as publisher of the books of the German travel and adventure author Karl May. Schmid became very widely known during the Fischer–Spassky match in Reykjavik 1972, where he was the referee. When a person occasionally did not turn up, when a game wasn't played, when there was no agreement, when different interests had to be attended to, when absolutely nobody could be given preferential treatment, then Lothar Schmid would often come into the public eye to explain the situation. Schmid did that well, because he has by nature the appearance and manners of a diplomat. A good referee does not stand out, but is always present. As soon as there is a problem with lighting or the sound level or the temperature (a chess player in a poor position tends to be bothered by such things), the referee is called. He then tries to solve the problem in such a way that the opponent won't have reason to complain, just in case the game suddenly takes a different turn. For appearance's sake, he fiddles a bit with a tube, or a knob, and most of the time that is sufficient to settle the complaint. Once the player sits down and concentrates on the game, everything around the board disappears. The historic match in 1972 was saved above all by Max Euwe, because his authority was accepted by both camps. Lothar Schmid had to take care of the everyday problems; and because the match finally came to a good conclusion, he is able to cherish his contribution.

Our interview with him took place in Frankfurt, during the Book Fair.

Was it difficult to be a referee in Reykjavik?

Yes, very difficult. A lot of prestige was at stake. The whole world was playing: East against West, and I stood in between. An enormous honour, but a heavy one. Bobby was always difficult, but he was allowed to be difficult because he happens to be a genius. But so is Boris. He just is a much less complicated person; Spassky on the other hand carried the political burden with him. As representative of the Soviet Union, he was not permitted to lose.

What problems were there?

There were a lot of problems. It started with the preparation for the match. There was the so-called Amsterdam Agreement, in which all the conditions of the match were laid down – for instance, about the chess board, which had been created by an Icelandic artist. We also looked at the chairs of both gentlemen. I had chosen 13 different chairs from a furniture shop in Reykjavik, but Bobby did not think a single one was suitable. He wanted a leather swivelling chair from the United States. Boris then wanted one of these too.

Just before the title match was about to start, Bobby wanted to have an extra house in addition to his hotel room, that he would be able to retire to. That could immediately be taken care of – and also for Boris.

The Russians arrived at the appointed time, but Fischer did not come after all. He kept on making new demands. An English banker by the name of Slater then shouted: 'Come out, chicken.' He doubled the prize money, which had been fixed at $125,000. People figured that it was just a question of money. Bobby then finally came to Iceland, although a week late. I am glad that I was able to cooperate with Max Euwe, then president of the international chess federation. He was such a great personality. We succeeded together in calming down the Russians. The match could then finally begin.

What were the circumstances like in Iceland?

We played in a large sports hall, with 2500 spectators. There unfortunately was no carpet, so it was noisy; you could hear people walking around. We tried to fix that. Indeed we did our very best to make it as comfortable as possible for both players. Fischer could, for instance, become quite vexed by the crackling of sweet wrappers. We therefore saw to it that they only sold unwrapped confectionery at the box office.

There was, however, a large source of unrest in the hall. In front of the podium a tall metal tower with cameras had been erected that belonged to businessman Chester Fox, who had obtained the film rights to the match. This tower was movable, so that the chess players could be filmed from all sides. That could not pass muster, that bothered Fischer. Maybe he lost the first game because of it. He blundered, and captured a poisoned pawn on h2. It was a Bishop endgame that normally would have ended in a draw. Fischer tried to give a bit of colour to the game with this move, but it turned out completely wrong. He lost and was looking for a scapegoat. That became Chester Fox and his camera crew. We had thought of something else for the second game in relation to those cameras. They would be set up next to the podium, but Fischer saw the lenses, and they were too much for him. He wanted the cameras removed altogether. Otherwise he would just not turn up. But the cameras were mentioned in the Amsterdam Agreement and he had agreed to that, so we let the cameras stay.

The procedure in chess is that the clock is activated [at the time appointed for the match to begin] and the players must be present within the hour; otherwise they lose by default. I pressed the clock of White for the second game. Bobby had White in this case. He should have been there but he wasn't. We tried our very best to get him to the playing hall in that hour. He was in his hotel, but he didn't want to leave it and he wouldn't come. The clock ticked on. It was so tense. Half an hour, three quarters of an hour passed by; no Fischer. We finally tried to organize a relay-race of police officers and attempted to coordinate all traffic lights from the hotel to the playing hall so they would all show green. He didn't come. It was such a tragedy! Bobby was behind by 2–0. The whole match was at risk.

His lawyer Marshall came on behalf of Bobby to the organization prior to the 3rd game. He proposed that the next game be played in a 'separate room'; then Bobby would come. But the rules said that one should only move there in case of severe disturbances. He said: 'Then you will have your disturbance. I shall take a sledge-hammer and destroy the playing table.' Absolute madness. I could of course have said that I had not heard this or that Fischer was now completely finished; but I talked it over with Spassky. He said like a real sportsman: 'Yes, we'll play in the small room.' That was a very noble gesture, but also very tragic, because Fischer won the 3rd game as Black.

Something else happened just before that game. There were closed-circuit cameras in the small room through which the public could follow this game by a relay in the main hall. Fischer wanted to have these removed too. I said: 'Bobby, you must play here.' Spassky said: 'It is now or never.' While they were both a head taller than me, I took them by the scruff of the neck and put them in their chairs: 'NOW YOU PLAY.' And by a miracle Spassky made his opening move. That was a tremendous relief. But it was also a deeply tragic decision of Spassky, as he lost the match in the end because of this. Unbelievable. Chess history was being written at that moment. Spassky did his duty as a sportsman and lost the 3rd game.

Fischer had won, so the tension was back a bit. The 4th game ended in a draw, Fischer won the 5th, again as Black. Boris played weakly, he could not control his nerves. The 6th game was also won by the American, and that is when Fischer took the lead. A few great games followed, but it quickly became apparent that Boris was too nervous. A pity, but that is a part of chess. You have to be able to deal with the tension.

Is it correct that the Russians started to become difficult?

Certainly, yes. You have to try to be in their position. Their top player was not doing so well. They wanted to check Spassky's swivelling chair. It came from the United States. Spassky had played weakly, so they thought he had been influenced by something in the chair. They were looking for drugs or a chemical mechanism. We allowed it and the chair was subsequently dismantled. There was of course nothing wrong with it. They also checked the lighting. The lamps were alleged to irradiate something or whatever. They found three dead flies.

How did the 21st game, the last game, go?

Bobby had a good position. He only needed one more point. The game was adjourned. The procedure is as follows: the person due to move next [after the adjournment], in this case Spassky, had to record a move that was then sealed in an envelope by the referee. I was called by Spassky the next day. He had studied the position and did not see a way out. He resigned. That was the conclusion of the match. Fischer appeared in the playing hall. However, I still opened the envelope, but simultaneously announced that Spassky would not appear any more. Bobby did not know what to do with himself. I shook his hand; he was world champion. I realized that it was a great tragedy for Spassky. A day later, during the final celebration, a fine thing happened. Both players were analyzing all kinds of positions on a pocket chess game during the festivities. That says everything about the match. Despite the turbulent circumstances surrounding them, the two men had become friends.

Twenty years later you were also the referee in the return match between Fischer and Spassky in Montenegro. How was that?

I had originally said no, but the organization made me change my mind. I still went to the first game. On the way there I flew over war territory. You could hear them shooting down below. Quite extraordinary. Sveti Stefan, the peninsula where the match was played, was so beautiful that I stayed longer. I flew back after the 7th game. I later also attended the second session, in Belgrade.

Bobby won justly in 1992. Look, Spassky had not played much in the previous years, and we did not know a thing about Fischer. Fischer's genius was clearly still there. He had aged quite a bit. He had a beard and was raving just like before. It was a great event. There were 150 journalists. Fischer could have been a bit more diplomatic during the press conferences, but that is the way he has always been.

Fischer was a real chess artist. The first game in Sveti Stefan was splendid. Chess can sometimes give you aesthetic pleasure, certainly Fischer's games. It is only a pity that Karpov and Kasparov never played against him. Maybe Fischer was indeed afraid of them. They were both of course very good. It is a real pity; it could have been so beautiful.

Do you know where he is at the moment?

The rumour is that he is living on some island between Japan and the Philippines. That could be true. No idea. I haven't had contact with him for over ten years. I hope he is doing well.

Hans Böhm

Hans Böhm's greatest contribution to chess was the public interest in the game that he managed to generate and maintain among the Dutch public over a long period of time. The foundation for this general interest was laid by Max Euwe in 1935, and it was later fuelled by a Dutch potential world champion: Jan Timman. Several elite tournaments were staged in the Netherlands. Böhm wrote and presented programmes about the game during those tournaments in which he took part himself, and he gained his own best results in the period 1974–85, but from 1985 onwards he committed himself to a career in the media.

A remarkable aspect of his playing career was that his results as an international master were better than his objective strength. This was due to a combination of good concentration, an unusual opening repertoire, and a remarkable preference for the endgame. He was more of a player in general than a chess player in particular.

Böhm presented the radio programme *Man en Paard* (Man and Knight) under the inspiring direction of Jos Timmer for 13 years, an unprecedented run for a programme about a game with such a small following. Already, back in 1975, he had begun to report on chess developments for the radio sports programme on NOS, *Langs de Lijn* (Along the Line). From 1980 to 1990, he also wrote a twice-weekly teletext report about the world of chess. Böhm covered all the World Championship matches for Dutch television from 1978 to 1993, when Kasparov brought about a split in the chess world. He presented many chess courses; he made the last of these in 2000 in the persona of Count Schakula (a play on the Dutch word for chess – Schaken – and Dracula). Böhm twice set a world record in simultaneous display, in 1976 and 1987 (on the latter occasion playing 560 opponents in 24 hours, winning 94 per cent of the games), and he still uses simultaneous display as a means of publicizing the game. He also advises organizations on chess events, as he did during the memorial tournament in Curaçao in 2002.

Tell us about your adventures in 1972 in Iceland.

I was then 22 years old, and in my own way professionally occupied with chess. I wrote about chess, and I played in pubs and clubs. I had the feeling that I had to be there. It was a historic match. I was in Amsterdam. I bought a return ticket to New York with a stopover in Reykjavik; that was much cheaper than a round trip to Reykjavik. I got myself a visa for the USA, hitch-hiked to Luxembourg and bought a standby ticket. Quite a few students did that sort of thing. It was quite a cosy congregation at the airport. And at a certain moment some seats became available, and we left for New York.

I pretended to get sick on the plane, something to do with my stomach. I got out during the stopover in Reykjavik, I was 'too ill' to continue the journey. When the plane left, I obtained a tourist visa for Iceland, and then I headed for the match. I was prepared to do anything to attend the match.

I slept the first night in the toilet-cum-bathing area of a campsite, which had been erected especially for the event near the playing hall. I even tried to barricade the door in the morning. All those people who had to pee and who were taking showers – that bothered me! I later made use of the hospitality of certain Icelandic ladies. Look, when you're 22, that's a *fine* way to travel the world!

How did you get into the match?

I had the membership pass of my Rotterdam [football] club Xerxes with me, and on top of the strategic spot where it said 'football club', I had stuck my photograph. I thought: those Icelanders won't notice that. I just said that I was a journalist – and it worked! They did not check these things fanatically. So I was able to walk around in the rooms where the Russian and American seconds kept office too, right in the middle of where it all happened. That was nice.

Did you attend the entire match?

I hadn't left home until the animosity surrounding that second game – Fischer didn't play – was over. The question was whether the entire match would continue at all. Maybe Fischer had gone mad. So I considered the risk too big. But when the third game was being played, I knew that I could go to Iceland. Eventually, I attended the ninth to the 21st games.

What did you think of Fischer during the match?

Impressive! – that is, except for the first game, which he lost because of a ridiculous blunder. The rest was impressive. His winning score was completely deserved: 12½–8½, after falling behind by 2–0. He was clearly superior. Look, just before that he had won against absolute world-class players like Larsen and Taimanov with a score of 6–0. That is, frankly speaking, an impossible feat. He deserved that world title completely. I really did not begrudge him the title one bit.

What kind of chess player was Fischer?

A purist. Fischer was also crystal-clear in his analyses. There was not a single weak spot in his reasoning. The power of simplicity. That was impressive. He belonged to a different category. Take Botvinnik, who played with very profound concepts, all of it completely prepared in his living room, almost scientific. Then there was Tal, who was frivolous. He sacrificed pieces when he honestly did not know what the consequences were going to be. He was an adventurer. Karpov is a prophylactic kind of player, a spider. You have chess players who play the game of a cobra, like Capablanca did. But Fischer, yes, he played crystal-clear, very lucid. He was unique in that regard.

What do you know of his youth?

Fischer was an exceptional case. When he was 13 years old, he was already popularly destined to become world champion, you could see that. He obtained results that were not possible at his age. He had an encyclopedic memory. He played endgames in which he had to play the 15 best possible moves in a row to win, and he would do so without effort. He put things on the board and demonstrated performances of thinking power and calculation ability that were unique. It is therefore logical that this influenced his character, because he was so young and had already gained so many fine results. Of course Fischer was pigheaded, but how could he not be? I guess there was also a lot of comment about Rembrandt and Dalí too. I do not think this is so unusual.

What was the finest moment in Iceland?

That was the moment of the finale. It was the 21st game. It was adjourned. Spassky could have drawn by sealing the right move. This move was written down and saved in an envelope by the referee. Next day the game was resumed. It was due to begin at 2pm, and the whole playing hall was full of people. The question was whether Spassky had sealed the right move.

The clock was started by Schmid. For the first half an hour nothing happened. Fischer wasn't there, Spassky wasn't there, the clock was running. The playing hall was buzzing: what was the matter? Then Fischer entered the stage. The envelope was opened at that very moment – those are the rules. The move was carried out on the board. It was the wrong move – Bishop d7 – and simultaneously the referee, Schmid, announced to the public that Spassky, because of this move, had phoned to resign, and that Robert James Fischer was therefore the new world champion.

Fischer stood on the stage: a bit gawky. Such a round of applause descended on him from the playing hall that he did not know what to do with it. He was used to silence and thinking. And there he stood. I clapped in front of the podium until I had blisters on my hands, not only for that world championship, but also for everything that he had brought to us: the splendid Sicilian openings, the victories of 6 to nil, you name it. We were applauding his entire career. Because he did not react, the waves of applause kept coming. You wanted it never to stop. That was the most beautiful part of the match.

And yet it was to be his last match for 20 years.

Something snapped in his mind. Each world champion has always rested on his laurels. And rightly so: the road to the world title is long and hard, and when you have reached your goal, you are allowed to sit down on the throne and enjoy it. Then you want to show who you are and what you are capable of for a period of time, until you are challenged again. Everybody respects you, you travel all over the world. Fischer is the only world champion who did not make use of that privilege. He did not grant himself that pleasure. He has not played chess since 1972. Yes, only once more, in 1992 against Spassky. That controversial match in Yugoslavia that was paid for by war profits. He should not have done that. But that is neither here nor there.

Do they still talk a lot about him in the chess world?

You hope that he will come back, but you know that he is someone who has overstepped too many boundaries. He is *persona non grata* in his own country, he wanders around in Hungary and Yugoslavia because he cannot go back to the USA. Yes, someone like that is an outcast, a lonesome lunatic, someone who just won't do any more. You can't imagine him sitting in a tournament hall – 'Good morning. A cup of coffee?' – you won't see him do that. The lightness of daily affairs is wasted on him.

You would rather imagine him wandering along the highway and having brilliant thoughts. Or … maybe suicide, that could be a way out for him. I would almost be disappointed if he ended up OK.

Do you think he has a split personality?

Yes, there are two Fischers. The artist, the creative mind, the chess player – and the human being. The former creates beauty, he is brilliant, well-reasoning and intelligent, and the latter is narrow-minded, sick, not a hundred per cent there. These are clearly two different people.

I do not value him as a human being, I don't care much about that, but I do value him as an artist. He has given me, as a lover of chess, so much beauty. The same applies to a football player like Maradona. What he does as a human being, that is something you can distance yourself from; but what he has accomplished as a sportsman is sublime, so perfect in its finesses. Fischer, Maradona, they were *so much* better than all those others who were also good. That appeals enormously to the imagination. That is why you can forgive Fischer a lot of strange things, but there are of course boundaries.

He became paranoid at a certain moment, started to hate Jews, accused people like Korchnoi of having made deals with Karpov. Completely senseless accusations, but you can forgive him that within the framework of the game of chess. Not within the framework of his being human; then they are reprehensible matters that he promoted, especially of late.

Fischer has always had enemies – sometimes people, sometimes countries. He actually attacks history. World War Two turned out completely differently according to him – you are probably well aware of his deranged thoughts. Denial of history, that is not a captivating characteristic. I do not have a good feeling at all about Fischer as far as that is concerned; but as a chess player, you should judge him on what he did for the game. He brought in professionalism, he raised the prize money enormously after 1972, he created a gigantic interest in chess. All those demands he made for better conditions in the playing hall, all those matters improved by leaps and bounds because of Fischer. You should not deny that even if he became crazy afterwards.

The demands that Fischer made for the match in Iceland were logical, even if they were strange – for instance, the ban on stiletto heels in the tournament hall. Fischer said: 'Women on stiletto heels are to be officially refused entry to the playing hall.' Of course the clicking sound of heels irritates – certainly on a wooden floor. It's quite annoying, but to think of demanding 'no stiletto heels' as a rule is rather strange, though it has logic behind it. Another one was: 'No children are allowed into the hall, unless they can play chess.' That is quite exceptional. It means you have to put a guard at the door who says: 'Hey boy, what is the Sicilian opening? OK, you can go in!' Yet Fischer demanded it. That demand was in itself logical, because children get bored, start to play games, and might walk around making a lot of noise. But he was the first one to think of something like that. He also considered the prize money too low. That had to be raised. But Spassky profited from it too, so he did not only do this for himself. He did it for the game of chess, and that was his great contribution.

Anatoly Karpov

Anatoly Karpov (born 1951) learned to play chess at the age of four. He was selected at age 13 to study chess under the tutelage of Botvinnik. It is safe to say that his strength increased in a straight-upwards line until he became world champion in 1975, when Fischer refused to play. His chess style is pragmatic and prophylactic: he does not want to crush, but only to win with as little energy as possible. Every counterplay, however small, is nipped in the bud. His opponents often resign because of a lack of good moves. Because the title was handed to him by default, Karpov won during his period as world champion (1975–85) everything that could be won – as if he wanted to prove something. In his career as a whole he has won a record number of tournaments: more than 150. His most bizarre match was the one against Kasparov in 1984. Whoever got six wins would be champion, draws not counting. Karpov warded off the brilliant, fiery force of Kasparov in the beginning phase with steady play. He was leading 5–0 after 27 games in, but the final, decisive win didn't happen. The match was abandoned, with the score at 5–3, after 48 games and half a year of play, by the controversial action of the president of FIDE, Campomanes – the only time such an event has happened in chess history. In 1985, Kasparov challenged Karpov again, and this time won. 'I gave him free lessons,' grumbled Karpov. By 1990 they had played more than 100 games against each other for dominance of the chess world. Those were unusual trials of strength, because they had such different styles, yet were so comparable in strength. Karpov is also politically interested; he is the chairman of the Russian Peace Foundation. His stamp collection also seems to be unique.

The conversation with Karpov was recorded in an Amsterdam hotel.

When did you meet Fischer for the first time?

I met him in 1972 when he was already world champion. But I followed his games prior to that, of course. Especially when he started to win one game after another during the candidate matches. I analyzed this period in his life and his games again recently. I now have a different view than I did at that time. Then we were very impressed by the big scores he made, but now I find more mistakes than I could find then.

So he made mistakes?

Yes, but he had a lot of energy and a lot of knowledge, so his opponents were afraid of him.

Was he the most brilliant player?

That's always difficult to compare. I think it's not correct. Every player is acting in his own time. Now we have more knowledge. If we start to talk about brilliance, then we have to start talking about [the 19th-century American player Paul] Morphy.

What do you remember of Reykjavik?

I was involved in the last training session with Spassky. But then the sport authorities in the USSR decided I was not high-ranking enough to go to Reykjavik. I didn't get permission.

We were following the games with the team that was preparing for the Olympiad in Skopje. Fischer was the strongest until game 11. I remember that from that point, I thought Spassky could have won every game, but he lost his self-confidence and then he started to make crazy mistakes from a winning position, like giving up a pawn in one move, or similar mistakes.

What was the reaction in the USSR that an American was World Champion of chess?

The official reaction was a big shock; chess players understood that Fischer could beat Spassky even though Spassky was leading in the personal score against Fischer [i.e. in their matches up to that time]. But all the games were big fights, and at that moment Spassky didn't work that much. I must say that he worked hard for only a very short period of his life. He has great natural abilities, he understands chess very well, but with Fischer it was not enough!

In 1975 it was your turn. How did you feel about the fact that he didn't defend his title?

Of course I was preparing. I did a lot of work. On the way to meet Fischer I beat the greatest players of that time. I beat Polugayevski with a great score. I achieved three wins after eight games. Then with Spassky I won four games after 11, so that was also halfway. Then there was a very long match against Korchnoi, which was very tight. In the end I achieved three draws to beat Korchnoi. So they were the strongest players besides Fischer. It means that I was ready.

Fischer had his personal problems, I believe. He was not ready. And I don't want to claim that he was afraid of me: most probably he was afraid of himself. So he became World Champion, he gave some interviews, and he believed that the World Champion has no right to make mistakes. And then with such a position and with such an outlook, you cannot play chess at all, because you cannot avoid mistakes. There are big mistakes and there are small mistakes. Big mistakes of course are not for a World Champion, but small mistakes you always make. It can be one, it can be two or it can be more. But to avoid mistakes altogether you must simply stop playing chess.

He made such an extreme task for himself that he couldn't start a game. As a champion he couldn't even start one game. So this was his personal problem, and I regret that such a thing happened to him. The chess world missed another great match.

What conditions Fischer asked for in 1975 were unacceptable for you and FIDE?

It was a thick book of rules. Some articles were reasonable, no kidding. It's important what light you have. You're sitting in one chair for 5 hours. So you must be comfortable. Good lights, whether there are shadows or not. The rules were quite good. Now they don't use these any more, and that is bad.

Fischer demanded a big advantage for the defending champion over the challenger. The biggest advantage he wanted was, first, to play until 10 wins without counting draws, which could have been a very long match. He only lost two games per year, so did I. How to do that? But still under pressure from the European and American Chess federation I accepted that, though I didn't agree with it. But then Fischer demanded another thing. We play till 10 wins, but in case of reaching a score of 9–9, the world champion keeps the title. In reality it means the challenger must win with a difference of two points. Even a difference of 1 point is big [at this level]. To win with two points is incorrect. I couldn't accept that, the chess world and the federation didn't accept it, and so Fischer used it as an excuse not to play.

You met him in 1975?

No, in 1976 and 1977 we had several meetings, but at the end of these meetings I just left with the conclusion that Fischer would not play. In 1976, I was hoping that he was coming back, but the last meeting in 1977 was strange. We almost agreed on everything, and it was an open question: what should we call this match? At that time in the Olympic movement they didn't recognize professionalism in sport, and because of this the Soviet Authorities had the same opinion. Chess was always [considered] part of sport in the USSR, and so I knew that the name Fischer had in mind – 'World Professional Championship' – [would be a problem]. I said we must exclude the word 'professionals'; the whole world will understand what we mean anyway. I explained [my reasoning] straightforwardly. In the beginning he was beginning to understand, but then when we had a written agreement ready, and the pens in our hands, Fischer started to sign and then he said 'No, No, we shall sign for everything, including the title, or we sign nothing'. Then I said to him: 'I had many problems the first time, in 1976 in Japan, I was accused of being a traitor.' Some people said that I wanted to sell the title – that I wanted to get a lot of money to play Fischer and give him the title back. Some stupid things they made up. But it worked. Then in 1977 I said we could change the title. But then Fischer didn't want to use any other title. Then I realized he just didn't want to play. He was in the same position as in 1975: he was looking for excuses to get out.

He was a coward?

I wouldn't use that word. He was not afraid. He was afraid to start the competition, he was afraid of his form, I don't want to say he was afraid of me or anybody else.

Would you like to play him?

He is still interesting. People are wondering what condition he's in. He's 60, which is quite an age for a chess player.

Is it possible to be absent for 30 years and play at the highest level?

He played Spassky after 20 years in 1992 and so he beat Spassky 10–5. A big difference but Spassky was not a big player any more. As we know from close friends of Fischer, he is still watching and analyzing chess. Fischer is more educated than Spassky, but still this match produced at least two very exciting games. But unfortunately the other games weren't great, because at least one of them [Spassky] was not thinking as a chess player any more. Most of the results were weak, but two games were on a very high level.

Fischer said that the Russians played pre-arranged matches.

We don't have this information. The only thing that happened in the past, and which Fischer probably always had in mind, was not pre-arranging the results or players just giving points to each other. The only thing that happened, which has been proved by the players, was at the tournament in 1962 in Curaçao – that Petrosian, Keres and Geller agreed [to produce] three draws in the first three rounds. With draws you cannot win the tournament [laughs], but this was a fact. Fischer played in Curaçao, and then he explained his bad play was because of this agreement. But Fischer took fourth place and had no chance to win the main place to meet the champion. But he had found an excuse for his bad performance.

In 1992 he was accusing you and Kasparov.

Nonsense!

What do you think of his situation right now?

I'm not completely aware of what he is saying. He always took a radical position. You can agree with him or not. He has the right to his personal opinion. He is not so educated that he can give comment on world policy, but he has his own experiences. I don't agree with some of his statements, especially about what happened in New York; that was a terrible thing. But what is quite clear [is that] the world is going down a very strange path. Modern democracy is not ready to meet extremism and terrorism. World leaders must think very deep and hard how to solve these terrible things we have now in the Middle East, in Kenya [the 1998 U.S. embassy bombings]. Of course it disturbs us very much.

Do you think he'll play again?

It's quite clear that he won't play again within the FIDE framework.

How do you feel about never having played him?

It's a pity. I was serious when I met him in 1976 and 1977. I thought at that time that it would be very interesting and very exciting.

Arnfried Pagel

Arnfried Pagel (born 1940) is a special person. He was born in Germany and set himself up as an engineer in the seaside resort of Bergen (in the Dutch province of Noord-Holland), where he had previously spent his holidays. He had the patent on an indestructible kind of concrete. Because of the threat of nuclear war during the Cold War, he started selling underground shelters. Pagel wanted to become a member of the local chess club, but his background caused problems. So Pagel started his own: the Koningsclub (King's club). He began to invite grandmasters from all over the place to play in it.

A new club, however strong it is, has to start at the bottom of the competition, according to the regulations. The results in the first five years were therefore invariably 10–0 in favour of the Koningsclub. Opposing clubs found out, however, that it was very expensive to have grandmasters return for an adjourned game, so many completely lost positions were not resigned by opponents who wished to hold out for a draw. Pagel was therefore prepared to pay a contribution into the opposing club's fund if, for instance, their player was a Queen down and was willing to resign before time-control. This made Pagel a controversial person. According to people who did not like him, he was a mad fantasist; to his supporters, an original tycoon. In 2001, he was invited to feature in the TV programme *Het Zwarte Schaap* (The Black Sheep). It became apparent during that broadcast that feelings about him had still not quietened down, even after 20 years. It is however a fact that Pagel visited Fischer – there is a photograph to prove it. What exactly took place is unclear.

Arnfried Pagel was interviewed at his home in Berlin, Germany.

How did the Koningsclub come about?

I like playing chess, and I decided at a certain time to go and live in Bergen. I knew that village well because I always went there on holiday. When I moved there, I became a member of the local chess club. But I was a foreigner, a German, and I was not accepted. They twice blocked me from playing in the first team. I then felt compelled to start my own club. Not a small one: I wanted success. That became the Koningsclub.

I am number one in the world in the field of concrete. If you are big in the business world and you are pursuing your hobby, you want to do it successfully too. We had to start in the lowest division of the competition, but we were of course much too strong at that level. It still had to be done that way, because we wanted to go to the top and you have to fight hard to get there. Look, a match is a match and you must always try to win it. That is how we finally reached the top.

You recruited only grandmasters for your club. Did you therefore try to contact Fischer?

No, he did not fit into the pattern. It was actually Fischer himself who made the approach. Alburt, a Russian grandmaster who had moved to the USA, played in my team. He had a friend who was in contact with Fischer, and I heard through him that Fischer wanted a bit more contact with the outside world and also wanted to play again. I wanted to bring Fischer to the Netherlands to finally play against Karpov, or to play a return match against Spassky.

It was 1980. I had to go to the USA on business, and decided to visit Pasadena. Fischer was living in some kind of sect, a foundation. I was received there and you might say I was psychically x-rayed. I am able to tell my story very well and I am very civilized. The people of the sect therefore believed me immediately. They brought me in contact with Bobby. He came all by himself to my hotel and introduced himself. He had become old in his face and he had a beard. I would not have recognized him.

I ended up staying for a week and met Bobby a lot in that period. We always made appointments on neutral territory, in restaurants. Our meetings there were a kind of Olympic hiking tour. He was very athletic and could walk unbelievably fast for a long time.

He used all conceivable ways to make himself as invisible as possible. He would walk through bushes in order to get onto another street, sometimes in daylight, sometimes in the dark. Let's say that he behaved like a person who thinks he is pursued. What struck me in those restaurants was that he drank a lot, but only water. He also ate a lot and clearly enjoyed it. Everything that was left over, he would take out in a doggy bag.

We had many conversations. If you want to get through to Bobby, you actually have to split him as a person. On one side there is Mr Fischer, and on the other side is Bobby. You do not get in touch with Mr Fischer; too many conditions are attached to that. That is doomed to fail. I therefore directed myself more to Bobby, and how he was put together. Look, he is a chess player. That reflects itself in the way he speaks and in his behaviour. He behaves like a Bishop, thinks quickly like a Knight, is solid as a Rook and he still retains the overall view of a King. If you approach him in that way, you will quickly come to a conversation.

What were all your conversations about?

Just about everything. The people of that sect were surprised that someone could come so close to him, but that was only because I took him seriously, allowed him to have his say, listened to him. He was very open. It was quite interesting. The stories that he is so negative about the Jews, I have to contradict those. He is indeed very interested. He was curious how I as a scientist could explain how Jewish people live so long. According to him, they can live 800, sometimes even 1000 years. Look, that is his opinion. You cannot start laughing about that in his presence. Such an affront would spoil everything.

He was, for instance, also curious to know how one could travel into the future by means of those so-called time-machines. I luckily found a good excuse. I said: 'Listen, I am working on it, but I can now only go to the future; how I can come back, I do not know yet.' He wanted to be kept up-to-date about the developments. I know for sure that he was seriously thinking of travelling into the future.

Still, you did not succeed in bringing Fischer to the Netherlands!

It came down to lack of time and because I had not prepared myself well enough. The second conversation took place in 1982, but that one was much too businesslike. It did not succeed.

Although it was very nice, you could call it a failed investment.

Did you pay him?

No, there were then stories that you had to pay inconceivable amounts, like more than a million dollars, just to be able to talk to him. But he is creative and so am I. When two creative people meet, then money is not important. Ideas are much nicer than dumb money. If he had come to the Netherlands, I indeed should have had to pay. But that would have been relatively cheap, one-and-a-half to two million guilders. That could have been earned back. Even a loss of half a million, I would not have minded at all. I mean, it would have been a magnificent experience. I would gladly have paid money for that. What else is money for?

Are there any tangible memories of your meeting?

We wanted to take photographs of Fischer, but that proved difficult. He never took the same route to the hotel I was staying at. I even hired a private detective. He would be paid if he could produce photographs. He did not manage to do the job. Not a single photo. That man worked for nothing for days. My niece had come along too. We hid her in a waste container and when Fischer arrived at the hotel, she secretly took some shots from under the cover. She later took a few in the street. They were pretty good. Unfortunately they were destroyed at a fire in my factory. They were in an album along with a letter from Karpov. All gone.

Did you play a game of chess with him?

Yes. That was a great honour for me. I lost 9–1. I won a game against him using the Dutch Defence. But that is normal; if you play ten times against someone, then you will always win one. That was of course a unique experience. It belongs to my most impressive memories.

Jan Timman

Jan Timman (born 1951) is heir to the legacy of Max Euwe, the only world champion the Netherlands has so far produced. Timman's father, a mathematics professor, initially wished his son to have a sound education, but Jan preferred the free life of a chess player. His profound game and his impressive successes removed all doubt. Already at 25 years of age, he was able to compete with the top players in the world. Times are changing quickly, because at the super-tournament of Linares in 2003, the 15-year old Radyabov beat Kasparov. From 1975 to 1990, Timman had the nickname 'The Best of the West', or jokingly, 'The Best of the Rest', because only Karpov and later Kasparov outplayed him. Jan Timman is one of the few top players who occupies himself with writing chess studies, creating exceptional positions with amazing dénouements. That is a time-consuming occupation, and only suitable for players of an artistic temperament. Remarkably enough, Timman is also a good blitz chess player, in games that total from 5 to 30 minutes reflection time. The honourable comparison with Max Euwe goes even further: Euwe became president of the world chess federation, FIDE, at the end of his active career; Timman was one of the initiators of the GMA, the Grandmaster Association, an organization for the top professional players. And while Euwe produced practical textbooks, Timman is chief editor of *New In Chess,* a highly valuable magazine that comes out six times a year, in which all the top players analyze their games extensively. *NIC* is acknowledged worldwide to be the true voice of the chess community. Jan Timman is a good example of the classic chess player.

Jan Timman never played Fischer, but he has met him. During their meeting in Brussels, they not only talked about chess, but also about Fischer's antipathies. Timman is co-author of a book about the American. Our interview with Timman was recorded in Willemstad.

What is your opinion of the scandalous things Fischer says over the airwaves nowadays?

I think it is a real pity. After all, Fischer is a sympathetic person by nature. He is always honest, he never minces his words. In general, the things he shouts can be logically explained, although some of his ideas are very bizarre. The result is that the logical part does not really take centre stage.

What do you know about his youth?

He comes from Brooklyn. He spent his youth with his mother and his sister and dedicated a lot of time to chess. He also likes pop music; he is for instance a great fan of the Bee Gees. He did not really receive any further cultural education, and the Soviet players often teased him about that. They said, for instance, 'Hey Bobby, would you like to meet Goethe?' (of course, he did not know who Goethe was) – those kinds of childish pranks. He did not like that at all, but his moves speak for themselves. These were weak attempts to put him in his place. I can imagine that he became annoyed by it.

How important was that victory in Reykjavik in 1972?

What Fischer did there had not only to do with chess. It was the story of a lonely hero who overcomes an entire empire. It is something that appeals a lot. I mean: Fischer even received a telegram of encouragement from Kissinger.

When Fischer was involved, there was always something interesting going on. He once even played a tournament by telex. That tournament, the Capablanca memorial, took place in Cuba, and the USA did not allow him to go there. So he played by telex. That in itself was interesting, because he was very much against the Soviets. He later hated and detested the Americans too.

With Fischer, matters are all so politically charged.

Correct, but I would have preferred it if he was still seriously involved with chess rather than with this peculiar nonsense.

Do you still take him seriously?

No, nobody can take him seriously any more. The remarks he made after 11 September are such crazy statements that you cannot take that seriously.

What did you think when he went off to play Spassky again in Montenegro, even though the US government had strictly told him not to do so?

I understood what he meant by doing it. Look, he had already wanted to play in South Africa prior to that. Not because he was such a racist, but because he was looking for countries on which sanctions had been imposed by the United Nations. He thinks the UN is against him, so Yugoslavia was to his liking.

He wanted to make a point?

He indeed wanted to show something. And he also gave Spassky a return match into the bargain after all those years. He [Fischer] still thinks that he is the world champion, because he has never been defeated by a challenger. As I already said, there is a certain logic in it. It is bizarre, but on the other hand, why not? I also met him myself in 1990. That was very interesting – it was in Brussels.

With Bessel Kok. Who is that?

Kok is an old friend of mine, whom I first met in 1985. He has done a lot for chess. One of his wishes was to make contact with Fischer. In that he succeeded with the assistance of Spassky.

How did that meeting go?

Fischer was registered under the name of Brown in the Sheraton Hotel. I met him at Bessel Kok's house and we later went to a restaurant. He looked rushed all the time, but he was very interested in what I thought about his ideas. He asked me what I thought of the Ivanchuk–Kasparov game. He still calls Kasparov Weinstein. If he does not like someone, then that person is automatically a Jew. We were sitting in the back of a car, very uncomfortable. He had a pocket chess game set with him and showed a position from that game. I had to think about it for a moment, but he said: 'I spent eight hours on it on the plane, just leave it.' His analyses are still high-class.

Where it went wrong was that he thought that everything that Karpov and Kasparov had done was a put-up job. That was really impossible, but he was convinced of it. The interesting part was that he tried to prove it through short draws. He said: 'Look, Weinstein is now thinking that he has to make a bad move, because then it will be a draw, and that is what he did.' But Fischer underestimated his own knowledge. Because *he* saw that it was a lesser move, but Kasparov hadn't. Kasparov offered a draw because he was so disappointed about the bad move he had made.

I wanted to discuss a Rook endgame with him too. I had analyzed that endgame well, but he then came up with a suggestion that I had not taken into consideration. That forced me to look at it again later in my hotel room; very interesting.

He is Jewish himself and still does not want to be associated with Judaism.

He was of the opinion that Judaism was a faith and not something you were born with. You can think about it like that. The fact that you are automatically Jewish if your mother is Jewish was not to his liking. That is also remarkable; that of course is related to the idea that you can never be 100 per cent sure who your father is.

Was the intention that there would be a match in 1990?

No, we did not discuss that. We only analyzed matters. I wrote it all down immediately. I am still very happy about that.

What does it mean to you that you were able to exchange ideas with Fischer?

The most interesting was that I had once dreamed about meeting him in a nightclub. That happened, because we indeed later went to a nightclub. Funny, I had never entertained the hope of meeting him. When I broke through internationally, he had just stopped. I played in 1972 in Skopje in my first Olympiad and he was then active no longer. This was a dream come true.

Is he the greatest player ever?

Yes, I think so. He stopped just at the right time. That second match against Spassky, in 1992, was not convincing. Kasparov has now also performed quite badly – against Kramnik. As far as I am concerned, Fischer is the best ever. It is a bit mortifying for Kasparov.

He can't stand that?

No, because Fischer was never beaten. He had a career which was not so long, but that has its advantages.

How great was his influence?

Enormous. He stimulated professionalism in chess. Spassky said once: 'Without Fischer there would not have been Karpovs and Kasparovs.' Before Fischer arrived, the communists were at the top, and they played for free. They received a state stipend. Fischer was a real pioneer. The amounts [he demanded] actually weren't that high. Then Karpov made it a habit of arranging high starting fees. That was of course not permitted in the Soviet Union then, so he told them [tournament organizers] to pay him in, say, rare postage stamps rather than currency. And that was permissible.

Fischer was the turning point?

Absolutely. Fischer was an all-round professional. He did not need anybody, he knew how to develop his own ideas, had a very versatile repertoire. He was a self-made man. When Fischer was young, he once spoiled an endgame. Olafsson, the Icelandic grandmaster, said then: 'Bobby, your opponent would have played this and that move, and you would have lost.' Fischer was very impressed by that. From that moment onwards he started to involve himself deeper in endgames. That was very important; he learned from his mistakes. That is why he became so good later on. No one can fathom the game of chess completely at a young age. It requires a lot of study. Fischer was unbelievably good and industrious in this respect.

Look, Fischer is someone who is a legend. More and more new strange stories are told about him. He is someone who appeals to the imagination. It is just as if the man once existed, but shouldn't any more. That is what it comes down to, but he is still walking around somewhere, at the moment in south-east Asia. He is occupied with Fischer Random Chess. That is a pity; he keeps himself busy with all kinds of theories about what the world should be like. And that is not going to cheer you up.

The United States and the Jews are the bad guys.

Yes, in this case his hate has shifted from the bad communists, the Soviets, to the Jews and American politics. He was always picking on the Jews, that was clearly a case of self-hatred. Now suddenly the Americans are the bad guys. The situation in his mind has changed. But well, what can you do about it? Nothing.

Dirk Jan ten Geuzendam

Dirk Jan ten Geuzendam (born 1957) is joint chief editor, with Jan Timman, of *New In Chess* (*NIC*). Ten Geuzendam takes care of reporting, the background stories, and the interviews. He is the sincere amateur, and so walks in the footsteps of illustrious predecessors like Evert Straat and Herman Hofhuizen. It is precisely the distance that he keeps from normal chess thinking that make his reports so valuable. Chess players generally enter a restaurant in sequence of playing strength; that is how the hierarchy works. Dirk Jan does not suffer from that constricting sense of admiration, and speaks freely with the entire elite. In his capacity as a reporter, Dirk Jan travels the world, following the special events. *NIC* is read in more than a hundred countries. It is now a smooth-running magazine, its roots going back to the 1970s. *NIC* is the professional successor to the popular Dutch chess paper *Schaakbulletin*. Chess players would call each other every name under the sun in its pages. If you were not insulted, you did not count. *NIC* is now the favourite magazine of the entire chess world, and all the grandmasters contribute to it. From the Letters to the Editor it is apparent that many people read *NIC* from cover to cover. Besides the magazine, which provides reading pleasure for every level, there is the Yearbook, in which the best games are brought together and classified. Links to all tournaments in progress can be found on the magazine's website at www.newinchess.com.

How popular is Bobby Fischer?

Enormously. He has not been active for so long, but still receives a lot of attention. He still clearly has an enormous attraction outside the chess world too. Everybody has heard of Fischer. Within the chess world he holds a mythical place because of his results and his personality. And outside it, he is also a plain myth, because there is so little known about him. When you go to a party and you say you are doing something in chess, there is always this question: 'What's up with that American, Fischer? Is he doing anything yet?' He is very popular.

You met him. Tell us?

You've got to be a bit lucky in these things, because you can't approach him. When he started to play again in 1992 in Montenegro, I was wondering whether we should go there. I did not believe it [would happen]. They should start playing first. In the middle of those deliberations, a fax came in at *New In Chess.* It asked whether we could provide Fischer with all the games that Spassky had ever played. It was the beginning of the era of the database. We had a very good system at *New In Chess.* At the bottom of the fax was Fischer's signature. This was *the* great chance to get in contact with him. We put all the games on a diskette and I went with them to Sveti Stefan.

It was rather difficult to get there, because of the war in Yugoslavia. I first flew to Budapest, from there by bus to Belgrade and then by domestic flight to Montenegro. The destination was slightly bizarre. It is a small castle. This was transformed by Tito into a tourist paradise for his most loyal aides. It is very beautiful, but in the middle of nowhere. There were banners in the street saying 'World Championship of Chess'. All quite unreal.

When I arrived, the fifth game had just been played. There was a strange atmosphere in the playing hall. Fischer had objected to the public [being there], and they had therefore built a glass wall. The result was a kind of factory hall with a suite, and Fischer and Spassky were playing behind it. Even if you were only whispering in the playing hall, one of these gorillas would approach you and say that you should stop or be thrown out. Mr Fischer might be bothered by it.

He lost the game he was playing when I arrived. I did not think it then an opportune moment to contact him [directly]. I wrote him a letter announcing that I had arrived with Spassky's games. I gave that letter to Torre, Fischer's Filipino second. After that it was a question of waiting. I was called at 11 pm, and Gligoric, who was a friend of Fischer's, was in the lobby. He said that Fischer had received the letter and wanted to meet me. I was confused. I said: 'Just say when – tomorrow at lunchtime?' He replied: 'Well no, now.'

I went down straight away. The atmosphere was a bit Hollywood-like. A black limousine was waiting there. We kept meeting several guards on the way who had to open barriers. They were also driving far too fast. We finally arrived at Fischer's headquarters, where we first had to load the files into his laptop. That took a bit of time; after that we went to see Fischer. It was all a bit unreal. We walked to an apartment, the door opened. I expected first a hallway, but we were in the room straight away. And there was Fischer. He had become older, heavier, had a beard and behaved awkwardly. He stood up to welcome me. He gave the impression of being ill at ease. He was clearly not used to being visited.

I gave him the print-outs and he really jumped at them like a hungry adolescent devours a Big Mac. That was going well, until he saw that the pages weren't numbered. The way in which he commented on that, with such a loud voice, made it at once clear to me that not all was well with this gentleman. Torre said, like a father: 'We can number them ourselves.' That was a good plan. But where? At the bottom of the pages maybe? Problem solved. Fischer then suddenly asked: 'With what colour pen?' It was then completely clear to me that he had become different. They finally decided to use a black pen.

We got to talking. I had the latest numbers of *New In Chess* with me, and a Yearbook. He looked in it and we then ended up talking about one of his obsessions. He considered it a rather good magazine, but it was too pro-Russian. Although ... there had been a good story in it, in which Kasparov accused Karpov of buying games.

He had two great obsessions: the worldwide Jewish conspiracy, and the Russians who fixed all games in advance. He went on and on about that subject. I maintained that he could not prove that. But he said that he had studied it for one and a half years and that he would write a book about it. He gave two examples, the first one even more complicated than the second. Finally I said: 'You heard the first rumours about fixing of games in advance in New York in 1990, but you state that it has already been going on much longer.' Then Gligoric said: 'O dear, the penny is starting to drop. The gentleman starts to understand.' But what about Korchnoi? I asked that because Korchnoi had been opposed to the Russian system. Korchnoi is also guilty, according to Fischer, and even Spassky. He was extremely serious about it.

Did you interview him?

I had a tape recorder with me, but I didn't use it. There was a threatening atmosphere. The organizer, Vasilyevic, walked around proudly showing that he had a pistol; the bodyguards were not exactly nice either. You really had to watch out. I started to ask Fischer a few questions at a certain moment. He then said: 'I am not going to give you an interview.' I thought for a long time afterwards whether I should write a story about it. I finally did compose a story about it for the *NRC* newspaper. This was after all unique; it was still a meeting with Bobby Fischer. That article appeared on Saturday, but I only left Montenegro on the following Tuesday. I was anxious that it might become known through Yugoslav connections that I had written about the meeting. I was glad when I was on the plane back.

Was it a chess match or a circus?

A circus! Apparently it was a dream of Vasiljevic, who earned his money in the weapons trade, to get this arranged. This was the only way, according to Kasparov, to get Fischer back behind the board: an insanely large amount of money ($5 million), in a country where things are not in order, with a financier who is very dubious. It was a small circus for a small group of Yugoslavs. The interested public from the rest of the world was kept at a safe distance. For instance, it was dangerous to take a photo of Fischer near the playing hall. Heavily armed, barrel-chested men were walking around, so it was better not to do it.

What kind of feeling did you retain from that meeting?

A feeling of disappointment. Before I went, I had three idols: [footballer] Johan Cruyff, [boxer] Muhammad Ali and Bobby Fischer. Here I saw one of my heroes, who was clearly sick, who had arrived at a phase of his life that you do not wish anyone [to be in]. It was humiliating. Simultaneously, there was the fascination of having talked with him. But the final result is still one of disillusionment. That he was in such bad shape.

I talk with a lot of grandmasters, but I had never interviewed Fischer. One's work as a chess journalist is really incomplete [without having done so]. Of course the thought occasionally occurred to me: 'Maybe I should go to the USA, look him up, explain my good intentions and then do an interview.' I always had this vague dream that I was going to succeed. But then nothing comes of it. And then through sheer good luck, you are suddenly sitting in Montenegro next to Fischer, but he is apparently paranoid. At the same time, he is someone who can be quite nice. I understand very well when people say 'Bobby is so nice, it is because of the bad outside world that he is hitting out at those around him the way he does.' That is another face of his. But in the three quarters of an hour I was with him, he changed moods constantly. One moment he was the angry man who saw conspiracies everywhere, and then really within half a second he switched and was at once interested, then you saw a smile that was attractive. But at the moment that you thought he was relaxed and you played along with that mood, he appeared to have jumped back into the other personality, the angry Bobby Fischer. I am convinced that he is a split personality, in which the angry side is gaining all the time.

Yasser Seirawan

Yasser Seirawan (born 1960) was a very promising junior player and is now a renowned grandmaster. But he never managed to break into that select group of serious candidates for the world title. He did not dedicate himself sufficiently to the game of chess to get there. Yasser likes jokes, and likes to tell jokes, and always sees opportunities for enterprise. He is a real entrepreneur, buying houses to renovate and then reselling them. Already in his chess career he has started a chess magazine, *Inside Chess,* that was read worldwide for a couple of years. Yasser used it to comment stubbornly on the many developments in the game. It closed down. In the heyday of the internet stock-market bubble, during the madness where companies that only existed on paper were quoted at 150 times earnings, Yasser attempted to make a deal to bundle together several powerful pillars in the chess world – magazines, tournaments, websites. He recently started publishing a series of teaching manuals, which were well received in the United States.

A plan was put on the table during the prestigious tournament in Prague 2002 to bring the many world champions and the various World Championship cycles back under the FIDE flag, and it was Seirawan who initiated this so-called Prague Agreement. Seirawan would be a good PR man for FIDE. His wife Yvette Nagel, who once played in the Dutch Ladies' Championship and who specialized in communications studies, is his solid support. Although the world chess federation abolished the requirement that its president should be a grandmaster, more areas of friction have surfaced under Florencio Campomanes (1982–95) and Kirsan Ilyumzhinov (since 1995).

Yasser Seirawan met Bobby Fischer during the return match against Spassky in Montenegro in 1992. They talked together for 11 hours. Seirawan got an idea of the way Fischer thought during that conversation. The interview with Yasser took place in Bled, Slovenia during the Chess Olympiad.

How big was Fischer?

It was a phenomenon. It really was. It was the time of the cold war, there was a race to the moon, Soviet–American military build-up and so on.

This was a game, chess, in which the Soviets had dominated. In fact there hadn't been a Western challenger since World War II – Max Euwe. Then along came this loner, this guy Bobby Fischer, who had some eccentric qualities, a personality, and suddenly he burst onto the scene. Suddenly everybody became aware of him. In 1972 in newspapers, magazines, radio, television, all media focused on this Cold War on the chessboard. Around the world the names Bobby and Boris were synonymous with the times, and his effect in the US was to create a chess revolution. Children from the youngest age, and also adults, had a fantastic interest in the game. I think in the US chess federation there was a fivefold increase in the number of members. All around the US, chess became visible. It was everywhere.

How old were you then?

Twelve years old.

Did you see it?

No, it was a little bit strange. I came a little after the bubble. I played chess that summer with a friend who was paralysed. He was a neighbour, and we played chess and other games. And suddenly I was told that Bobby Fischer was returning to New York, from winning the World Championship in Reykjavik; there was a ticker-tape parade. And I thought WOW, how great. We have an American champion. So I came along just a little bit after his victory, but I was swept up in it as well.

Was he as big a phenomenon as Muhammad Ali?

Yes, that is precisely the right analogy. He was really the Muhammad Ali of the chess world, the Michael Jordan of the chess world. He really had that name recognition.

And the money of course, because it was the US.

It was very strange because Bobby was not really motivated by the money. In 1972 he made all kinds of demands, which included the prize fund of $250,000. Today we think all our sport stars make millions, and they may not even be the best players in the world. And here was this guy who said: 'No, I want that amount of money.' And then in 1975, just to put that in perspective: after winning a match with a $250,000 prize, which he won 5–8 [the World Championship], in 1975 he was offered $5 million, and he refused!

So he didn't make the big bucks?

No. Normally, many of the sport stars get a salary from their sport, but where the windfall comes is from commercial endorsements. Bobby was offered, for instance, [a contract] to endorse Johnson and Johnson baby shampoo. It was a very lucrative offer, but his simple response was: 'I'm sorry, I don't use that shampoo!' So he didn't do endorsements either.

That's stupid.

I don't know about that, but it's simply remarkable that he refused time and time again to earn a lot of money. I think Bobby is a very pure person in that regard. Let us say VW came to him and said: 'Please Bobby, would you like to endorse our lovely car?' He would say: 'I don't drive. So I don't want people to think that I use that car when I don't.'

Not many stars think that way.

I don't think so either.

You met him once?

Twenty years after he won the World Championship, I met him in 1992 in Sveti Stefan.

Was that a dream come true?

Yes, because keep in mind: for me Bobby was always a hero. What he did was absolutely phenomenal. Virtually single-handedly he defeated the whole Soviet state, which was really aligned against him. Chess had some grandmasters in the US, but at that time it was just Bobby alone. The Soviets had teams of coaches and trainers and masseuses and cooks and psychologists and everyone, just to make their champions feel great, and Bobby was alone. So single-handedly he defeated that total system. So as much as for the fact of what he accomplished on the chessboard – and let us not forget his games were remarkable, they were perfect – what his victory actually meant was enormous, was so great. So for me as a teenager he was definitely a hero figure in the sense of a chess hero. In 1992 I got the chance to meet him and speak with him, so it was in a sense a dream come true.

How did you meet him?

Yvette and I were on the beach in Sveti Stefan, it was a rest day during the match. We were taking the sun and everything was fine. And Bobby came with his second Eugene Torre to take a swim. It was a wonderful summer day. And Yvette says : 'Yasser, Bobby is at the beach!' And I go 'OK.' Everyone on the beach had this awareness that Bobby was now swimming. And then Yvette said: 'Bobby is walking over.' Uh-oh. So [mimes increased heartbeat] Bobby is coming. I got up to meet him and he stuck out his hand and he really has big hands. In fact when we shook hands, mine disappeared in his. I was really shocked by the fact. He is a tall man, 6 foot 4, heavy, broad-shouldered, but really large hands. He says, 'I'm so happy that an American GM has visited Yugoslavia'. Keep in mind that in 1992 there was actually a civil war going on. Dubrovnik was 120 kilometres away and there was shelling. It was really a strange situation that there was a World Championship [going on] in a civil war.

Anyway, Bobby and I had a very nice discussion, and he invited us to have lunch in his apartment. We accepted happily, but before we had gone to lunch something strange had happened. Both Gligoric and Torre told me that Bobby was angry with me because I called him the ghost of Pasadena. He said to them: 'I'm no ghost, I'm a man.' So I thought, I have to clear this up right away. So I walked into his suite. Bobby stuck out his hands to say hello and as I got his hand I got a good grip and said: 'Bobby, I would like to apologize that I once referred to you as the ghost of Pasadena, and I'm sorry that I said that.' I could see on his face that he was not really happy with the apology, and that he was annoyed with me, but I didn't let go of his hand. He really had no choice, so he said 'Yasser, let's just forget the whole thing.' I said: 'OK Bobby!' I let his hand go and we went along wonderfully after that because I had broken the ice.

What did you talk about?

Well, first of all, it was one o'clock in the afternoon [when we arrived] and we spent the rest of the day there till midnight. So in 11 hours you can cover a lot of subjects. We covered such subjects as the US government, the Soviets, Kasparov, FIDE, his tax status, his unhappiness with the US judicial system, Jewish people, Bruce Lee movies, Seattle, Motown records. For me of course the most important were these subjects he spoke about very harshly. Specifically: Jewish people, the Soviets, and his relations in the chess world and with FIDE.

What is his thing with Jewish people?

This was a curious question, what the source of Bobby's *angst* is. Is he a Nazi? Is he a bigot, a racist, and how did that view evolve? I learned a lot.

No matter what subject you talk with him about his answers are: I really don't know anything about that. But if he starts talking about a subject, you notice that he knows an enormous amount, he really researches. We began from the fact that he was raised in New York City as a child. His mother left him and his sister alone at a young age. He was brought up by his older sister. So very little adult supervision.

Then he became a chess player and spent a lot of time in chess clubs. Chess is a sport that attracts a lot of Jewish players. Jews like education. Chess is really seen as an intellectual pursuit. So in almost no time his circle of friends were Jewish chess players. He enjoyed it. They helped him a lot.

When his career really took off, people came to him and said: 'Bobby, would you like to earn $100?' It was a lot of money, so he would do a simul[taneous display] for $100, and later he would find out that the organizer paid $400. He said: 'Wait a minute, I only earned $100!' 'Yes, but I asked you would you do it for $100 and you said yes.' That really annoyed Bobby because he thought that he was being taken advantage of. He began to memorize all these situations where he had been wronged!

This cumulated in the great match against Sammy Reshevsky [in 1961], who was a giant in US chess, and Bobby Fischer, which was organized by [Gregor] Piatigorsky in LA. He was a Jewish man, a famous cellist in fact. So during a very tense match, Mr Piatigorsky had a concert in the evening and he arbitrarily decided that the game should start in the morning so that he could go to his concert in the evening. Bobby said: 'No, I want to play during the scheduled time'. Mr. Piatigorsky said: 'I pay and I decide when you play.' Bobby said: 'I signed a contract in which it was stated that we play in the afternoon. That's what I'm going to do.' Bobby forfeited the game, and although the match was tied, Reshevsky was declared the winner. For Bobby this was a terrible blow. He felt wronged by this decision. Worse, in all the articles that followed, nobody blamed Mr. Piatigorsky; Bobby became the bad boy, the difficult person, who was making outrageous demands. Not at all! He had made an agreement. He wanted to keep it and suddenly he had to forfeit. And again this for him was a Jewish episode in his life.

In 1972 we have the famous case of Chester Fox. Bobby, who was very sensitive, heard the noise and he demanded that the cameras be removed simply because the contract said that if they were disturbing, they wouldn't be allowed. He said they were disturbing; they said too bad! He said I won't play; he forfeited game two. Then they removed the cameras.

And again this was a Jewish person, Fox, who had injured him. This keeps building up. Then he does research and find that he's not the only one with these kind of experiences. Then it goes out of control.

What did Fischer say about his hatred against the Russian Players?

This was actually the funniest one, because during Sveti Stefan Bobby said: 'The Russian players cheat. They, Kasparov and Karpov, have arranged every move of every game of every match. It was all a script.' He was certain that's what's happened. I was laughing. I said: 'OK, Bobby, suppose you're right. Just explain to me how they did it. Let's go to Sevilla 1987. It is 11–11 and two games to go. The players get the script, because they have to memorize what they have to play. And in the room down the hall you hear Anatoli Karpov cheer: "YEEAH, I'm the winner tomorrow!" And Kasparov: "Oh no, I've to lose game 23? Why?" But because they're good Soviet kids, they play the script. Right, Bobby? And then comes game 24. The Russian Commissar comes in the middle of the night and gives them the script and suddenly it's Gary who is the winner, it's 12–12. Kasparov stays world champion. And Karpov says: "Wait. I've always been a good communist, why is the Soviet state no longer supporting me?" This is how they do it, right, Bobby?' In the meantime all the people that were with us, we were just laughing because it was too funny. The image I was creating actually forced Bobby to laugh. He said, he didn't know how to react, because maybe he believes in the idea that you have to have a script. Somebody has to compose the game and somebody then has to tell the players they have to perform and act. It was very hard for him to give me details of how he thought it had taken place.

You could not make him change his mind?

I don't think so, but I could at least draw his attention to the fact that there is a certain falsity in his way of thinking in this particular issue.

What about the taxes?

Very clear. Again, Bobby had an agreement with Time-Life magazine in 1972. The agreement was very clear. There would be a reporter, Brad Darrach, from *Life* magazine. He would have access to Bobby during Reykjavik 1972. There would be a big story and Bobby would be paid. It was a significant amount of money. Bobby had only one condition: Both Brad Darrach and Time-Life would not publish a book about the match. Report for the magazine, perfect, but don't write a book because

Bobby wanted to reserve that right for himself. He would like to write a book about this match. It was in the contract. Then Brad Darrach wrote a book: *Bobby Fischer vs. the Rest of the World* [1974], entirely devoted to the 1972 match. Bobby was angry. So he went to Californian court, arguing violation of the contract and seeking a ruling that yes, Time-Life Warner has violated the contract, that they shouldn't print any more books, and that they should give him compensation. The case goes to trial and Bobby loses. I don't know the details, maybe this, maybe that; for Bobby this was a really terrible blow. He saw himself as the little guy versus the great media empire Time. That the judicial system exists for justice and it didn't give him justice. That really the odds are against the little guy, Time-Life had all of these lawyers, the big shots, the heavy hitters, and he was just alone. It was David versus Goliath, and David got crushed. So after this he said: 'Why am I paying taxes? I am paying taxes for a system that is not protecting the individual, which protects government and big business. I'll stop paying taxes.' It was 1976 when that case was decided. Till 1976 he was paying his taxes. Then in 1976 came the great breakdown with the judicial system and he said: 'OK, from this day on I don't pay taxes'.

Because he played in Montenegro, Bobby is not allowed into the USA any more. What do you think of his situation right now?

US President Bush [Senior, 1989–93] wrote a presidential decree aimed only at Bobby Fischer, saying: 'You're not allowed to play in Yugoslavia.' And Bobby went 'ppppttttt [points at his nose], I'll do it.' There's no warrant for his arrest. The taxes are a much bigger problem than the $10,000 fine.

It is a very sad, sorrowful situation. What Bobby did in terms of defeating the Soviet state was phenomenal, a superhuman effort. A remarkable effort. Since that time, from a hero of the people he has become an inwardly looking, bitter, very unhappy man, a racist for sure, a person who is now isolated from his own country. The man who was going to be the Muhammad Ali of chess quit, went into exile, a lonely life. A bitter person. It is very, very sad to see. If Bobby Fischer had died in 1972 after winning the World Championship, he would have died the happiest man in the world because he had achieved his dreams. From that time until today it has been thirty years of isolation, sadness, fear. He is afraid that people will take advantage of him, try to exploit his name and good reputation. Let me put that in perspective. During the years that

Bobby didn't play, he came up with a good idea. That for every move you get bonus time. It was so quickly adopted by the chess world. He patented the idea. Instantly there were chess clocks with the Bobby Fischer time-control mode. Millions of dollars are made which they happily ...! Bobby says: 'I don't want to go to the justice system because I can't get justice there.' So he has been exploited again. For Bobby it seems that the world is against him. He remembers every cut, but he doesn't remember every kindness!

Zsofia Polgar

Zsofia Polgar (born 1974) was part of the experiment of the scientist Laszlo Polgar. He has three daughters, Zsuzsa, Zsofia and Judit, and from birth they were brought up and trained to be women of genius. He wanted to demonstrate that you can educate each child, provided it is properly coached, to perform exceptionally. When Laszlo discovered that his children had a talent for chess, he elected to train them and develop their skills in that, because performances are easier to measure in the game of chess than in, for instance, mathematics. There are also few women who play chess at a high level – not even five per cent of the number of male players – so if all three of his daughters could advance to an elevated level, then the experiment would be deemed to be successful. There was a lot of opposition. The Hungarian Ministry of Education did not accept at first that the children would receive a home education. They were sometimes escorted to school by the police. The authorities started to sputter when the experiment became known worldwide. The name Frankenstein was used. Now, thirty years later, we have to congratulate Laszlo and his daughters without reservation. All three of them not only recorded historic results, but are also balanced, pleasant women. Zsuzsa became women's world champion, but was so disappointed at the reaction that she turned her back on the arena. Zsofia beat many a grandmaster, but dedicates herself currently to her young family. She had a baby in 2002 with her husband, grandmaster and practising doctor Yoan Kosashvili. Zsofia also thinks that the game cannot be a fully fledged fulfilment of life. The brilliant crown on the Polgar work is youngest daughter Judit. In 2003 she obtained a 2700+ rating, which means that she has become part of the absolute world elite.

Bobby Fischer was a regular guest in the Polgar home during his stay in Hungary. After a big quarrel, the Polgar family stopped all contact with Fischer. Zsofia took part in the chess event in Curaçao in 2002, and that is where we talked to her.

What is your relationship with Fischer?

At the moment, none. A few years ago I had the chance to meet him a couple of times. He was a guest in our house a few times, we played some ping-pong, went to restaurants together, him and my family. Until a point when he got very mad at me. The reason was very simple. I gave a simultaneous exhibition in an American Club in Hungary and he told me this was unacceptable because everything that has to do with the US is against him. He has all these theories of conspiracy, you know. He was an incredible player, but today he is not the Fischer he used to be.

He changed?

I didn't get the chance to meet him as a kid, but I grew up with his games. He was an absolute hero until I met him. He is still a hero, a chess hero, but I can't say the same about his personality.

What do you think of his personality?

[Laughs shyly] What can I say? He needs medical help. I'm not qualified to say it, but he could use some help.

What happened to him? How is it possible that he has changed so much?

I'm not the one to tell. That's more the field of psychology.

Is it because as a chess player he lives in isolation without people around who could correct him?

I don't know. He always had his weird things, but they still don't end up in such extremes as he did.

What was the role of your family when he entered Hungary. Did you help him in any way?

He didn't need help. We just had fun times together. Looking at some games, playing ping-pong and going to restaurants. It was of course very interesting for us in the beginning. He would tell us about his strange ideas, about his anti-Semitic views, which is incredibly strange because he knows we are Jewish. So it was a weird relationship. but we had some fun times together.

What did you say to him when he exposed his anti-Semitic views?

Well, as always with such a person, he said: 'It's not the personal, it's in general!' We just changed the subject when it came up. There is not much you can talk about.

Did you play chess a lot?

Not so much.

Why not?

We would have loved to play more. We played a lot of chess, but even when we played it was shuffle-chess [Random Chess], his chess. We also analyzed some ordinary games.

Was he the greatest player ever?

Well, I don't like to compare different players in different times. Morphy was a genius in his time, Fischer was obviously ahead of his time, but then again Kasparov is also a great player. I certainly like [Fischer's] play a lot.

Why?

There was an incredible harmony in his play. I like the openings he played. I grew up with some of them. Mainly the harmony of the positional structure and the attacking style. That's what I like about his play.

Do you think he'll ever come back?

I don't know. I think if there's enough money he probably would. At some point he will run out of money, right?

He earned a lot in 1992.

Yeah, but he spends a lot too. That's one thing I remember. If he goes to a restaurant, he is a huge guy, he eats the whole menu.

What did he say when you questioned him about the auction in Pasadena, and his anger at the USA?

I think it was a tax problem.

Do you know where he is?

Benkö said that he is in Japan. He is in touch with him; they're good friends.

You don't want any contact with him any more?

No. I'm not even sure that I'm glad I met him. You know, he was such a hero, such a great example from his games. Even if you read about these strange ideas, you don't always believe the papers, but now you have to face it. Now I have to separate the person and the chess player.

Those are two different persons?

Two different things, yeah.

Let's try to end positively. What was a positive thing about meeting him?

He's funny. He has a sense of humour, we had some laughs together. The most positive thing is his chess of course.

Nigel Short

Nigel Short was a prodigy. There is film of him in very short trousers, commenting on a just-completed simultaneous display. He was precociously wise as a teenager and he remained playful in later years. He would rather play on pinball machines or play guitar. He left textbooks alone, so the great promise he held was not fulfilled rapidly. It was too easy for him to coast along on his talent. He had a son at the age of 20, and then started really to work on his studies. In 1993 he became the challenger of world champion Kasparov by beating Timman in the final of the candidate matches. 'I see it as my task to use the individual way of thinking of the West European to beat the collective way of thinking of the Eastern European,' Short philosophized in advance. 'It will be Short and it will be short.' 'It *will* be short,' predicted Kasparov, and he was right. This match is, however, a stain on World Championship history because the players suddenly decided to play it outside the world chess federation, FIDE. They even established a separate federation for this purpose, the Professional Chessplayers' Association, with only two members. The reaction of the hundreds of colleagues all over the world was clear, because they never got an additional member. FIDE removed Short from the official rating list, which curtailed his invitations drastically. That is a hazardous situation for a professional. In the meantime the crisis has passed, because his name is reappearing here and there on lists of participants. Still, Short takes with him two pressing questions wherever he goes: Would the game of chess have been better off without his action in 1993? How much further would he have developed under a different regime?

Nigel Short wrote on 9 September 2001 in his column for the *Sunday Telegraph* that he had played against Fischer on the internet. He had such a bad beating in a couple of blitz games that the mysterious opponent could only be one person, he believed. This interview took place in Bled (Slovenia) during the Chess Olympiad.

You claimed that you played Fischer on the internet. What makes you say that?

Yes, well I was playing on the ICC, which is a forum for chess players, where you play blitz chess. I was there morning and evening. I was approached by somebody who asked if I would play a guest. Normally I don't do that. I like to know who people are. I was approached by someone, he actually was an international master from Italy. He said: 'There is somebody who would like to play you.' He said: 'I played him, and the guy beat the hell out of me. It might be interesting.' Somehow I was persuaded. He told me the guy would be back later that evening and would use a code word, so I would know it was him. I hung around for one hour but there was no sign of anyone that evening. I forgot about it.

A few months later, I was approached again. The second time I agreed to meet him. We started to play some chess. This person was very strong indeed. I was beaten quite badly. In fact I had just come back from the Olympiad in Istanbul. I was exhausted. This person approached me and used the code word.

Which was?

I can't remember. I do remember, but I'm not going to tell you. We played and I was beaten badly.

How badly?

I think I lost all my games. I think I played 8 games. Lost them all. That's not so unusual – it's a matter of form. If you're in good form then you can win a lot. In poor form you can lose. I'm not normally beaten so severely and I apologized for my poor play. And I had been chatting with him. This person was very polite and very funny. And I said maybe we could play the next day.

The following day I met this person and I had already recovered. We played and I won a couple of games, but overall I lost again very heavily. It was very interesting. The person was clearly a native English speaker, most likely American-speaking. He was a person with a lot of knowledge of the chess world. I kept dropping some hints as to the identity, without saying his name. It was a very interesting experience.

What kind of questions did you ask him?

Well, hmmm, there were all sort of things. We were commenting on games, I was asking him about his career. He said he was a retired chess player. We also talked about Tal.

I played him many times. You know that he called his sacrifice on E6 a *calling card.* That was the expression. So we talked in a sort of familiar way about certain people. Of course it was possible to fake, but ...

There was a combination of facts that made me think that this might well be Bobby Fischer. One of the questions I asked was about an obscure Mexican player. So I asked if he knew Armando Acevedo. The person just replied: 'Siegen Olympiad!' Which is of course where Bobby Fischer played Armando Acevedo. This reply came instantly. That was interesting to me. This was obviously someone with an encyclopedic knowledge of Fischer's life. When I spoke with Boris Spassky about it, he said: 'Oh, excellent question.' Some people have criticized me and said this was a weak question. They make out that Armando Acevedo is a sort of superstar. He isn't. He is very obscure. This very precise reply ... [even] suppose somebody knows who he is, would he know that they played each other in the preliminary groups. I think it was a good question.

But I think there were more things that made me believe that this was Bobby Fischer. I didn't say this to anyone for a long time, but I began to speak to other GMs. They had the same impression as me. There was one time in Brazil. One Brazilian GM told me about his experiences of playing an incredible player which could be Fischer. After this, I decided to publish this. It was inevitable that this story would come out sooner or later.

In January of this year he gave an interview on Icelandic radio and he said it was not him.

In the absence of other evidence I have to take his word for it. So it seems that most likely I was wrong. But the curious thing is, there are still a number of questions. What was this person doing? Let's say it's an American who has very good knowledge of computers, because he was not using a laptop. He must have been hardwired into the system. Because the moves came so quickly, you cannot use the primitive way. How do you do that? I don't know, he obviously was somehow using this analysis engine that was plugged into the system. So the guy must have some proper knowledge of computers, assuming it was a computer.

So you've got this guy with an encyclopedic knowledge of the life of Fischer, spending hours and hours over months playing random GMs. The point is, what sort of a person does these things? There are plenty of hoaxes. There is one guy in England who is very famous for appearing in a team photo of Manchester United. It's the nature of hoaxes that they like publicity when they can pull off a big stunt. Well, here there was no publicity. This was a guy who came on, who was playing as a guest, he asked me to come on and play as a guest. So you have guest A versus guest B. Nobody is watching. If I'm playing as Nigel Short there are usually dozens of people watching. If it's two guests there is nobody watching. What sort of a person is doing this? There are still unanswered questions. In the absence of any proof I have to take his word for it. Probably this is my Hitler diaries [referring to historian Hugh Trevor-Roper's authentication of notebooks purporting to be Hitler's diaries, which turned out to be fake]. I was wrong in my attribution of this, but it's an open case and I would like to know who this person is.

So what's the code word, what's his name?

No, I'm not going to tell you. A while ago I had the same approach again and I decided not to play, but maybe one day I'm going to play this person again. I never saved the games. I didn't know how to do it.

Is it possible that you played a computer?

That is most likely. If I had to bet on it.

Suppose it was Fischer, what does that mean to you as a top chess player?

It would be a great honour to play him. When I talked with Spassky about this, I said the guy seemed quite funny, and normal. Boris said: 'Well of course!' Because you always hear Fischer is absolutely barking mad. And maybe he's strange in many ways, but this person was very polite to me, obviously very articulate and good fun. I've played a great number of world champions and beaten them. There are some champions I have met but never played, including Max Euwe. Botvinnik was another one. That's a great honour. These are the chess gods.

Fischer is like Zeus, the god of the gods. Absolutely at his peak he was probably the greatest player of all time. Kasparov is playing better for longer. You cannot compare these guys. But Fischer, the guy was a genius. Of all world champions he stands out. It's a shame he went down the way he did. It's a shame he stopped playing. That's the great tragedy.

Eugene Torre

Eugene Torre was born in the Philippines. He is the only grandmaster of this island archipelago. His years at the top occurred in the period that his compatriot Florencio Campomanes was president of the world chess federation, FIDE. Torre is one of Fischer's best friends. He was Fischer's second in the 1992 return match in Montenegro. It is difficult to describe what being a second to Fischer means, because he has always played his own game and only trusts his own analyses. You get the impression that Fischer is more interested in the social abilities of those who surround him. In 2000, Fischer stayed for awhile at Torre's home in Baguio City. Torre arranged for a woman in that city to carry Fischer's child, so the genes of the chess genius would not be lost to posterity (see page 67). Every interview with someone from the small circle of friends surrounding Bobby Fischer gives problems. They know the price: too much inside information is not tolerated; the friendship may be stopped abruptly. Fischer keeps a strict line. What is needed in those conversations is the art of getting around the difficulties. You need to read through that when it appears on the page. Torre was approached with a hidden camera and a camera with a telephoto lens during the making of the documentary *The Wandering King*. We suspected that the meeting would otherwise be very short. The interview took place during the chess Olympiad of 2002 in Bled. What we cannot print here, unfortunately, is Torre's body language. The reader should use his own imagination. Think of someone who is afraid of someone he cannot see.

Since friends of Fischer are rather reserved when it comes to dealing with the media, we approached Torre during the Bled Olympiad secretly, and armed with a transmitter.

Mr Torre, I am from the NOS and we are making a program about Bobby Fischer. We would like to interview you about him.

I do not have any contact with him of late. Our friendship has diluted a bit. I do not know if we are still friends.

Is he angry? Disappointed in you?

No, it is not so heavy, but something like that. I think it is because I was president of the Filipino Chess Federation. We are again connected with FIDE and Fischer has a dislike for that body. I think it has something to do with that.

But do you know where he is?

I have an inkling, yes. He lived for a long time in Budapest.

Yes, I know that. Thereafter he lived for a while with you?

Yes, yes. He even gave all kinds of radio interviews there. Maybe that is of use to you.

Didn't you arrange those interviews on the Filipino radio?

Yes, because I thought it was annoying for him that his things in Pasadena had disappeared. So I helped him. It was not good what they did to him in the USA. Despite the fact that I knew that he would damage people in those interviews, I had to do it. It was really bad what happened to his things.

And now he lives in Japan?

He travels a lot through Asia.

Is it possible for us to get into contact with him through you?

I have to check that first through another friend. It will be very difficult. I'll think about it. What is it about?

We are making a movie about Bobby Fischer. He will be 60 in March and that seemed a good reason to find out how he is doing.

Hopefully you can then also talk about Fischer Random Chess. He is very busy with that at the moment. The pieces at the back are randomly placed by the computer into the initial position. I must say that I am also a great proponent of that chess system.

We would really like to talk about it with Fischer. We have sent him e-mails but he did not react.

I'll see what I can do.

But if you want to be friends with him, are you then allowed to talk with me about him?

Well, he expects it of me that I am not too open about him. I really have to think about it. Ask me tomorrow about it once more.

Next Day

Mr Torre, did you think about the interview as regards Fischer?

Tell me once more – what exactly you have in mind?

We are making a movie about Fischer and since you are (or have been) one of his confidants, we want to ask you a few questions.

When?

Well, that can simply be done here in the hotel tonight, for instance.

What are the questions?

I would dearly like to talk with you about your contact with him. What kind of person he is. What he is occupied with at this moment and so on!

Look, Fischer is a very social man. He is a good friend. He means well to everyone.

Except for the Jews then!

Are you going to talk about that too?

Well yes, that would be discussed automatically when we start talking about the Filipino radio interviews.

I do not think it is a good idea to do that interview. I really think that he won't approve of it. I am sorry. I am not doing it. Have a nice day and success with the movie.

RADIO INTERVIEWS

Over the past few years, Bobby Fischer has given 28 radio interviews (as of 20 October 2004). The first was broadcast on 13 January 1999 on a Hungarian radio station, while the most recent dates from just a few days ago from a Japanese jail facility, broadcast on his favourite Filipino radio station. When the original Dutch edition of this book was published, some 20 radio interviews had been broadcast. In the final chapter, we shall devote a few pages to his latest tirades over the airwaves (that is, those since his arrest at Tokyo airport in May 2004, at the request of the US authorities). He is being held there without bail. The compilation of quotes below are mainly a re-translation of the Dutch text. However, they are accurate in content. Fischer encourages anyone interested, however, in his latest broadcast of 18 October 2004, to listen directly to what he has to say. So – with due apologies – the following text has been prepared without checking against all the hours of sound files of these interviews, which are available directly on his website at http://home.att.ne.jp/moon/fischer/. All the broadcasts (except the first one, and two others from an Icelandic radio station in Reykjavik, the most recent on 23 August 2004), were made from several Filipino radio stations. See also the interview with Pablo Mercado in the next chapter.

Fischer has a couple of conditions for such interviews. It has to be 'live', there cannot be a single Jewish connection within the broadcasting station, and Fischer must be allowed to express his opinions and views freely. He decided to tell his story on radio after his belongings in Pasadena were auctioned.

All interviews have an underlying message: that Fischer has fallen victim to a worldwide Jewish conspiracy. Here are some passages from various tirades:

> 'What the hell is going on? I am bothered day and night by those Jews. I'll tell you exactly as it is. They want to lock me up, they rob me of all I have. They lie about me. I have had enough of all that shit!'

> 'Look what I did for the United States. There is nobody who has done more – all by himself – for that country than me. Until I won the world title in 1972, it was a football and baseball nation. Nobody considered it an intellectual country. I changed that all by myself. But now the Cold War is over and they don't need me anymore. They want to destroy me.'

'You got that arrest warrant against me; they say I am not the world champion anymore; they stole the royalties of my book (*My 60 Memorable Games*); they faked that book. They made the CD-Rom *Bobby Fischer Teaches Chess* illegally and without paying for it; they stole the patent of my Fischer clock. It just does not stop. They even made an illegal movie, *Searching for Bobby Fischer* [1993]; everybody is abusing my name. Now there is a new thing, they are now stealing all I have.'

'I paid for 12 years the cost of that storage space in Pasadena until I was blue in the face. Those damned Jews have now stolen everything. It was worth millions. There were so many tremendously valuable things there. A letter from President Nixon, all the stuff from Marcos, his letter inviting me, things of my mother and sister, my photo album, a telegram from Kissinger, posters, books, files, contracts. Those damned Jews stole everything.'

'It's business as usual for the Jewish liar, embezzler and thief Bob Ellsworth. For this hardened, heartless Jewish criminal robbing all of Bobby Fischer's belongings in storage was a "piece of cake". Like taking candy from a baby. Hardly worth losing any sleep over. As a Jew he is convinced of the superiority of his "race", and even more importantly he knows that the fix is on and that the police won't touch him!'

As you may recall in about late 1998 or early 1999 the US government, Bob Ellsworth and Bekins Moving and Storage company (Pasadena, California branch) plundered all of Bobby Fischer's cash valuables and other belongings (including his gold and silver coin collections) which Mr Fischer had kept in storage at the Pasadena, California branch of Bekins Moving and Storage company for many years.

However, it should be pointed out that Bob Ellsworth was a very wealthy man even before he entered into the above-mentioned conspiracy to rob all of Fischer's belongings at Bekins!

For example, for well over 15 years now Bob Ellsworth (Robert D Ellsworth) and another man by the name of Bob Kuhn (Robert L Kuhn) are the partners and co-owners of the Professional Cassette Center.

'It is quite simple. There are three Jews responsible for this theft. The first one is Bob Ellsworth, my agent in the United States. He forgot to pay the bill, while I transferred $5,000 every year to him. He lied on the phone, because he alleged that he had paid. The second Jew is Bekins Storage. They allege that I owe $480 and that is why they auctioned all my things behind my back. The third Jew is the American government that thinks this is completely legal. That is how it is.'

Transcript from live radio interview number 5, broadcast on 10 March 1999, in Manila, Philippines:

'And I'm asking, you know, I was reading in the papers about this guy Osama bin Laden. I read this about a month ago in the *International Herald Tribune*, that he is looking around, he's scouring the world for good Israeli and American targets to hit, you know? So, may I humbly suggest Mr Bin Laden, you hit Bekins'. You know? Hit Bekins and Mr Bob Ellsworth!

'I cannot go to the judge [courts], because the Jews control the courts in the USA. That is really a wash-out. I was in the past involved in several court cases. It is one big joke. The United States are ruled by circumcized Jews.

'It is one big conspiracy against me. Those f**king bastards are trying to capture dominion of the world. They have invented that story about the holocaust and the gas chambers. There wasn't a holocaust at all in World War Two. They are filthy liars!

'What do I have against the Jews? They have something against me!

'Jews use Christian children. They murder them and use the blood for their black magic ceremonies. They mix blood through those crusts, the matzos. They eat them when they celebrate Pesach.'

On 11 September 2001, just after the two planes hit the World Trade Center, Fischer himself called Radio Bombo. He wanted to give his reaction:

'This is all wonderful news. F**k the USA, f**k the Jews. It is time for the United States to have their head kicked in. I want the United States wiped out! Once and for all! What goes around comes around. The United States and Israel have been murdering the Palestinians for years. Nobody is bothered about that.

'I am hoping for a totally new world. The United States should be taken over by the military, all the synagogues have to be closed down, the Jews should be arrested, their ringleaders executed and apologies should be made to the Arabs.

'I say: death to President Bush, death to the United States, get rid of the Jews. Whine, you cry-babies, your time has come. Hallelujah!'

On 29 January 2002, in an interview with Icelandic radio, Fischer was asked if it was correct that he was secretly playing chess on the internet:

'That is bullshit! That is a Jewish lie!'

But Nigel Short says that he played against you through a computer.

'He can say whatever he wants. It is not true. I do not play classical chess any more. That game is totally played out. That chess is dead! Many games are pre-cooked by the computer.

'Someone should ask Kasparov about my charges that his first match was prepared move by move, and then put him through a lie detector. You'll see he is lying through his rotten teeth. He is a goddamned liar, Kasparov, he is a criminal.'

Pablo Mercado

Pablo Mercado is a presenter with Radio Bombo in the Philippines. He conducted 13 live interviews with Bobby Fischer between January 1999 and September 2001. Fischer used language that was abusive towards the Jewish people, the Russians (particularly Gary Kasparov) and the United States.

This interview with Mercado took place by phone.

Tell us a bit more about your radio station.

Radio Bombo is a local station in the city of Baguio. We belong to a large network of 43 local radio stations, and so cover the whole country.

How did you make contact with Fischer?

He often called himself, but the first time the contact was made by Eugene Torre, the chess grandmaster who lives here in Baguio City.

Why did Fischer choose Filipino radio stations to broadcast his opinions?

Fischer told us that he chose us because the media in the Philippines are not controlled by certain groups of people. What he meant by that was the Jewish people. According to Fischer, the Jews control the media in the United States. That is why he does not give interviews there. He can talk here freely about his anger against the USA.

What do you think of that?

I think that he should be able to say whatever he wants. The media are of course free in many countries, but well, that is his opinion. That is allowed.

What precisely were the most important issues in those interviews?

The reason why he gave interviews was that in 1998 things belonging to him and stored in Pasadena disappeared. One of his friends who should have paid the annual fee for the storage space had forgotten to do it. Those possessions of Fischer were auctioned without his permission. He says that those things were worth millions. According to him, the Jews were behind it. They conspired together with the government of the USA, and he wanted to reveal that on the radio. He was incredibly angry.

You also talked to him on 11 September 2001.

Yes, he himself called just after the news of the attack on the World Trade Center broke. He said: 'Pablo I want to be in the broadcast!' I asked him why and he answered that he had a lot of things to say. He thought that the Americans had themselves to blame for it. That is what I can recall. He really enjoyed it.

Did you ever meet him?

Yes, several times. Especially in 2001, he was a regular visitor to our city. He visited the Philippines regularly in that period. He called me and asked if I had time. He was our guest in the studio a couple of times. I think I met him personally six times.

Where did you meet him?

Here in Baguio City in the country club, once at Torre's home, and a few times in the radio studio.

What did you think of the person Fischer?

He really is a brilliant person, but indeed very eccentric. Look, that anger against the Jewish people and the United States is insane, but as a chess player he was of course fantastic.

How did you feel about meeting him?

Very excited, but I sometimes got worried about his anger attacks. The intensity of it, not normal. You can have a real good talk with him, provided you have the same opinion.

Did you toady to him? Are you also an anti-Semite?

No, no. I just nodded a bit like that, but I did not tell him that I was against the Jews either.

Is Fischer popular in the Philippines?

He is very well known here. He has become reasonably old. He has a beard, he is slightly balding, so people do not recognize him. We often went to restaurants and nobody knew who he was. What was striking was that he talks very loudly. Not normal, what a passion he has.

David Barnouw

During one of his infamous interviews with a Filipino radio station, Fischer was asked since what time did he know that the Jews were targeting him. He answered that this had become clear to him when he read the book *The Secret World Government* by Count Cherep-Spiridovich in 1977. He then knew 'for certain' of the existence of a 'worldwide Jewish conspiracy'. We went to the Netherlands Institute of War Documentation (NIOD) to find out more about this anti-Semitic literature, and talked there with David Barnouw.

What kind of book is The Secret World Government*?*

It is one in a series of publications beginning at the end of the 19th century, in which the theme is that there are people who are bent upon gaining world domination. That is to the detriment of the rest of us; Spiridovich was a Russian, but it also concerns the white American. The Jews and the Bolsheviks are conquering the world. The idea is that if you deny it then you are stupid, because they have already done so; but it is so secretive that you and I have not even noticed.

What can you tell us about the writer, Spiridovich?

He was a Russian count. He was an anti-revolutionary, he belonged to the losing side during the Russian Revolution. He went to the United States, and that is where in 1926 he wrote some 200 pages. We do not have it in our library. You can only get it through the internet. In summary, it's very similar to *The Protocols of the Elders of Zion.* That is maybe the best-known booklet of its kind. It describes how the Elders of Zion, a group of Jews, are busy in gaining world dominance. That booklet originates from German, French and Russian ideas and brief essays of that time. They were distributed at the beginning of the 20th century, but it quickly became apparent that it was all fiddlesticks, stuff and nonsense.

Is it an invention?

They are purported to be minutes of a secret meeting that took place in

Basel in 1880. It was supposed to be a kind of board-meeting of a large Jewish Limited Company in which they discussed how they were going to dominate the world. There is not the slightest proof that this meeting ever took place. The booklet is anyway unreadable, but it still seems to have had an enormous influence. It is likely that it was written by the Tsarist secret police in order to increase latent anti-Semitism among the Russian population. The population was already in revolt against the Tsar; they tried to bend that anger and aim it in the direction of the Jews. It did not stop the Revolution, but people still thought: 'You see, it is true what that booklet says. The Jewish communists are taking over the reins of power.'

Fischer said that the scales fell from his eyes after reading this literature.

If you are already anti-Jewish and you believe in plot and conspiracy theories, then that could be possible. I mean, there are parts of the United States where they believe that things are often not what they appear to be; that strange machinations are at work. The subtitle of the book by Spiridovich is, for that reason, 'The Hidden Hand'! Anti-Semites think that you are very stupid if you do not believe that. There are also people who believe in Martians.

Searching for Bobby Fischer

When Fischer disappeared in 1972, all chess lovers were left behind in growing amazement. What would happen to the beautiful works of art we were hungering for? Fischer was the best, but he was still so young, he could still surpass himself. How can an artist who eats, drinks and lives his art, stop just like that, all of a sudden? Isn't that contrary to all human instinct? Rest on your laurels, certainly; many have done that. But now nothing at all?

The great void that Fischer left had to be filled one way or another. America was in mourning after Fischer's disappearance. In 1993, the movie *Searching for Bobby Fischer* was released, after the book of the same name by Fred Waitzkin. It is the story of a boy, Joshua Waitzkin, who is pushed to play chess. Not only are there constant references to Fischer's career in the film, but we also see him appear in authentic archive images. Fischer fans lean forward in their seats to grasp every second, every grimace of this footage. Fischer in Reykjavik, on TV shows, on a bench in the park, when analyzing a game, during a simultaneous display at 14 years of age. As a drama, the movie may provide a nice experience for a non-chess player: a small, brilliant boy is shown as having a human side too – unlike Fischer, the movie strongly implies. But as a chess movie, the errors are too disturbing, so that you never get into the story. The positions are incorrect, there is no real reflection time during the games and the moves are executed unnaturally. Sometimes 20 moves are made in quick succession, supposedly in a tournament situation. And the sequence of the positions is often not good. That you do not see the entire board, well, you are not going to fool a chess player with that. Fischer would never have given permission for it. Joshua also has a good trainer, played by Ben Kingsley. He takes the instruction of the little boy, who is still learning so much, ridiculously seriously. He does not allow Joshua to go to the park anymore where the 'kibitzers' have a lot of fun and play for a dollar.

Even if the technical chess aspect is weak, you taste the screenwriters' research from the pronouncements the trainer makes with great dogmatic assertions. They went through a lot of biographies – not only Fischer's – and collected a few things. Hans Böhm had some pithy comments on these:

Fischer discovered that chess is not a game and not a science but an art.
('More likely Tal would have said this')
Fischer looks at the game from inside out.
I want to have what Fischer took with him when he disappeared.
He is a young Fischer. ('An emancipation: "Fischer" equals genius')
You should detest your opponents. ('Fischer respected his opponents')
They hate you. ('Only the layman thinks that')
You do not know what a loss does to you. ('You learn from it')

When another father analyzes a position with his little boy just before the game, he says admonishingly: 'Capablanca would not have done that.' The location, the expression, as well as the supposed playing level of the pupil and the father, give to that kind of smart-aleck remark a different impact than it was meant to have. I could go on listing the dramatic false notes: children who look at each other for a long time before the game to intimidate; Joshua offering a draw for psychological reasons when he has a winning position against another boy; children toppling their King theatrically when resigning. But the authentic images of Fischer make up for it. He is sitting on a bench in the park, and is asked how old he was when he seriously started to play chess. Fischer thinks for a while and then says: 'I started to play chess seriously when I was seven', and he then laughs heartily. It is all about that laugh. Fischer understands that the interviewer had other things to worry about when he was seven, just like most children. Fischer laughs about his own situation; he is amused by how strange life can be. Fischer laughs at himself, but he could have been laughing at somebody else.

Appendix 1

EUWE AND FISCHER

Max Euwe (1901–1981), the only Dutch world champion, won his title in 1935 by beating Alexander Alekhine. In that period, the reigning world champion was allowed to select his opponent; if one could raise enough money (in those days, the equivalent of 10,000 Dutch guilders), one could play for the highest honour. In any case, Euwe had the greatest moral claim to challenge for the title; a match between the same grandmasters in 1926, only decided in the last game, was won by Alekhine with a score of 5.5–4.5. Remarkably enough, Euwe thought he had little chance in 1935, while on the other hand he expected to win when defending his title in 1937. History shows that the challenger has a psychological advantage. Euwe was an amateur, because his real profession was as a teacher of mathematics, and later a professor of informatics. He used his methodical approach when he wrote his standard work *Oordeel en Plan* (*Judge and Plan*); this was the first textbook used by Boris Spassky, among others. In 1956, Euwe began pioneering work in the use of computers. He was appointed professor in the methodology of automatic data conversion in the universities of both Tilburg and Rotterdam in 1964. He later became director of the information centre in Amsterdam. Despite his work in this field, Euwe was wrong in his assessment that the computer would never be a threat to the human chess player. He became president of the world chess federation, FIDE, in 1970. It was a flourishing time for chess all over the world. Euwe travelled to the most distant corners of the globe to promote the game. Thanks to Euwe, the Fischer–Spassky match did not end prematurely. According to the letter of the regulations, Spassky could have been declared the winner without even playing. Fischer, after all, arrived two days late. The Russians were angry – first demanding victory, and then apologies. 'What are two days?' Euwe replied laconically.

In 2002, *New In Chess* brought out an English translation of the 1972 book *Fischer World Champion!* (*Fischer Wereldkampioen!*), in which Max Euwe talks frankly about the organizational problems just before the match, while Jan Timman takes care of the analyses. Euwe covers at length the many meetings and exchanges of letters with the Russian and American camps. It was a nerve-wracking process to get Fischer to sit down behind the board, since he was someone who too did not allow for any compromise of his demands. Fischer's demand to raise the prize fund (which was $125,000) was granted at the very last moment by the assistance of the English banker Slater (raising it to $250,000). Spassky profited from this too, because the winner received 5/8 and the loser 3/8. In connection with the documentary *The Wandering King* (after which this book is titled), one journalist raised question marks about the role that Lothar Schmid, the referee in Reykjavik, had played in 1972. In fact, Euwe had already been clear about it. He finished his report with the words: 'The match finally started on Tuesday 11 July, nine days later than planned, but it would be more than worth our worries. When I left Reykjavik, I could leave the further developments with an easy mind to chief referee Lothar Schmid. He was not only fully authorized, but had shown himself in the previous days to be an able, diplomatic and utterly objective assistant.' Euwe therefore did not write anything about problems after the first game, which Fischer lost with a basic error, nor about Spassky's radical win by default in the second game, nor about the difficulties before game three. Timman starts his analysis of game three with: 'At five pm Fischer enters the alternative playing room. A short but vigorous discussion about the presence of a closed-circuit camera occurs. Anyway, Lothar Schmid succeeds in getting Fischer behind the board. The match can now start once more.' In short: Euwe saw to it that the match could start in the first place, and Schmid saw to it that the match kept going.

Euwe sums up all FIDE stipulations with which each organization for a World Championship from then on had to comply. A few of those stipulations give a better insight into Fischer's demands:

> The spectators must sit at a reasonable distance from the playing zone. [Fischer had demanded that the first seven rows would remain empty.]
>
> The public must maintain complete silence, and is not permitted to use any pocket chess sets. [Fischer had demanded a ban on stiletto heels and wanted children who could not play chess to be denied entrance.]
>
> The players' chairs shall be comfortable. [Fischer had demanded his own chair.]

The playing materials (board, pieces, clock) must be of the best quality. The board absolutely must not shine. [Fischer had immediately ruled out an artistic set that had been specially made for the occasion, and demanded different lighting.]

In his book, Euwe occupied himself also with the question: who is the best chess player in history? That question is often asked. It cannot really be answered, because you must compare playing styles and different times. In his 1955 memoir, *Meneer Caïssa, schaakherinneringen van Dr. Max Euwe* (*Mr Caïssa: Chess Memories of Dr Max Euwe*), Euwe takes the easy way out by mentioning only the strongest aspects of his contemporaries – Capablanca, Lasker, Alekhine, Botvinnik, Keres, Bronstein, Bogolyubov, Reshevsky and Maroczy. All of them impressed Euwe, and he did not want to have to choose between industry, talent, ambition, resilience and inventiveness; but also because one player 'may excel in one aspect and may fall short in another aspect'. Twenty years later, in 1975, Euwe however makes a serious attempt at answering the question in *Bobby Fischer en zijn voorgangers* (*Bobby Fischer and his Predecessors*), in which he takes a detailed look at Fischer's style and his results in comparison with the previous world champions Steinitz, Lasker, Capablanca, Alekhine, Botvinnik, Smyslov, Tal, Petrosian and Spassky.

Euwe uses the mathematical system developed by professor Arpad Elo in order to compare the results. The Elo system certainly offers a reasonable insight, because with the various Elo ratings in hand, you can predict a tournament result with 80 per cent accuracy. You can also use the Elo system to compare results in the past with results of today. By comparing the Elo ratings, Fischer scored in 1972 the highest of all, with 2785. So Fischer was the best. From the standpoint of 2004, Fischer would finish behind Kasparov in second place. But is that convincing? Fischer played relatively little, but his rating shoots up mainly because of his last four matches against Taimanov, Larsen, Petrosian and Spassky in which he scored 31 points from the official 41 games (the second game against Spassky, lost by default, does not count for the Elo system). If Fischer had played another tournament later and won it, the chances are that he would still not have complied with mathematical expectations. The ratings of the other participants would then simply not have been high enough. Fischer was, like Kasparov, far ahead of his time as regards Elo rating.

Euwe thought that the rating system itself was not enough, because 'the game of chess contains very many different elements'. Euwe preferred questions like 'Who is the greatest tactical player?' or 'Who is the greatest positional player?' or 'Who is the greatest all-round player?' Those are questions that can be discussed more rationally, Euwe thought.

The structure of the Elo rating system is roughly as follows:

1000 points = seeing a chess board for the first time
1500 points = playing a good game at club or regional level
2000 points = first and second division in national competition
2300–2500 points = international master level
2500 points and up = grandmaster level
2600–2700 points = top 100 players in the world
2700 points and up = top 10 players in the world

Who is the Best Chess Player of all Time?

Following is a list of all official world champions since the title was first used in 1886, with their estimated Elo ratings. One should exercise a great deal of caution in comparing the Elo ratings of players from different periods. Arpad Elo calculated these retrospectively in 1972 for chess players from the past; they were further adjusted by the present author in 2003.

1886–1894	Wilhelm Steinitz	(2700)
1894–1921	Emanuel Lasker	(2750)
1921–1927	Raoul Capablanca	(2725)
1927–1935	Alexander Alekhine	(2750)
1935–1937	Max Euwe	(2700)
1937–1946	Alexander Alekhine	(2750)
1946–1948	title vacant	
1948–1957	Mikhail Botvinnik	(2775)
1957–1958	Vassily Smyslov	(2700)
1958–1960	Mikhail Botvinnik	(2775)
1960–1961	Michael Tal	(2700)
1961–1963	Mikhail Botvinnik	(2775)
1963–1969	Tigran Petrosian	(2725)
1969–1972	Boris Spassky	(2700)
1972–1975	Bobby Fischer	(2825)
1975–1985	Anatoly Karpov	(2780)
1985–	Gary Kasparov	(2850)

In 1993, just before the World Championship match against Nigel Short, Kasparov established his own federation, the Professional Chess Association. By doing so, he placed himself outside the organized chess world. He easily defeated Short, but officially lost his title; his status remained unaffected. Fischer, by his own determination, attended to the interests of professional chess players. His prestige was so unusual that he could accomplish this. The professional players later united to defend their interests with respect to FIDE, which was becoming more commercial all the time. Organizations founded to defend the interests of professional players include the Grandmaster Association (GMA, 1986), the Professional Chess Association (PCA, 1993), the World Wide Chess Association (WWCA, 2000), and the Association of Chess Professionals (ACP, 2003).

A laborious period dawned in which FIDE introduced new structures in the world championship. Not only was the frequency of world championship challenges brought back from three to two years, but also the reflection time per game per player was shortened. This resulted in several more or less transient champions: a second title period for Karpov (1993–1999), Khalifman (1999–2000), Anand (2000–2002), and Ponomariov (2002–2004). The FIDE knock-out championship in June and July 2004 brought another surprise champion, Rustam Kasimdzhanov from Uzbekistan, who is scheduled to battle with Gary Kasparov in January 2005 in Dubai under the Prague agreement of May 2002. This agreement was signed by almost all the world's top chess players then present, and by the president of FIDE. It was meant to unify the world titles from 2005 onwards. Vladimir Kramnik won the PCA title from Kasparov in 2002, and successfully defended it in October 2004 against Peter Leko of Hungary, scoring 7–7 with a hard-fought win in the 14th game. Of all these players, only Kasparov, Kramnik and Anand have really distinguished themselves since 1993. Kasparov incidentally retained first place on the Elo list during that period, so that he can justifiably be called the best player since 1985.

As regards the Elo system and the accompanying all-time ratings, it should be mentioned that Elo ratings during Campomanes's term as FIDE president (1982–1995) were exposed to inflation. To promote women's chess, Campomanes gave all women who played in international competition an extra 200 points. In 1972, Fischer had – if we include his victory against Spassky – a rating of 2785. Fischer would have had a rating of 2825 under the new system.

About the World Champions

Steinitz was a founder, he experimented consciously. Lasker also was ahead of his time, like his friend Einstein. Capablanca did not bother too much about opening theory, but struck in the middle game and faultlessly finished the job in the endgame. Alekhine impressed as a strategist. Euwe was the master of tactics. Botvinnik ruled by methodical preparation. Smyslov won on intuition. Tal was brilliant in attack; Petrosian brilliant in defence. Spassky excelled in strategy. Fischer fought, devoid of style, by more or less finding the best move. Karpov smothered all counter-play. Kasparov is the first and the best of the computer era with a destructive knowledge of opening theories.

What criteria can be used to determine who is the best chess player of all time?

- The length of their reign? (Lasker, Kasparov, Alekhine)
- Their number of tournament victories? (Karpov: more than 150)
- The highest Elo rating at a certain moment? (Kasparov, Fischer, Karpov)
- The highest Elo rating over a period of, say, two years? (Fischer, Kasparov, Karpov)
- The highest Elo rating over a period of ten years? (Fischer, Kasparov, Karpov)

One would expect a world champion to win five and draw five out of ten games (scoring 75 per cent). If everything works out, he'll score a bit higher; if he runs into a spot of bother, he'll score a bit less. Tim Krabbé once calculated (in his book *Fischer,* 1972) the scores on this basis over a period of ten years for, among others, Lasker, Capablanca, Alekhine, Botvinnik and Fischer. He did indeed arrive at percentages between 70 and 80, in which Fischer scored highest with 78 per cent. Karpov was content with 75 per cent as long as he came first, and Kasparov here also vies with Fischer for first place. His first reaction when he topped 2820 Elo points was: 'So, now I never need to hear again that Fischer is still the best.'

But what criterion weighs heaviest? Is the maximalist better than the pragmatist? Is playing a lot better than playing a little? Is a long period of smouldering play better than a short burst of scorching brilliance? Is the lonely player better than the one who has the assistance of teams of assistants? Is the objective best move better than a lesser one that also leads to a win? Is professionalism better than amateurism? Is it fair to compare the computer age with slower times?

If we combine all criteria, seven names start floating to the top. In chronological order: Emanuel Lasker, Raoul Capablanca, Alexander Alekhine, Michael Botvinnik, Bobby Fischer, Anatoly Karpov, Gary Kasparov. The best player of all time must be among them.

Everyone is allowed to have their preference. We are not going to compare styles and times any longer, because when mathematician and ex-world champion Max Euwe says 'these factors nevertheless are not quantifiable', then that must be true. Euwe was so objective in the end that he – immediately, with an apologetic smile – ruled himself out of the competition: 'No, no, I am not good enough by a long shot' (in 1975, on the TV program *Sport Markant*).

All in all, according to the rules of what is reasonable and logical, and of course with a touch of feeling, I am asking you to consider placing, in any case, Fischer and Kasparov in the top three.

Appendix 2

THE FBI FILES

On Sunday 17 November 2002, a report appeared on the front page of the *Philadelphia Inquirer* saying that the FBI had kept an eye on the Fischer family for years. Bobby's mother Regina Wender had been suspected of spying for the Soviets.

The newspaper managed to lay its hands on parts of the file. Bobby too had been well observed; in particular, his trip to Moscow in 1985 started alarm bells ringing. They were afraid he would be recruited by the KGB. Not only was that not the case, but it quickly became apparent that he disliked the Soviets.

Regina was followed attentively for some 30 years. Her whole history was unravelled, her letters were systematically read, her bank accounts were checked and her neighbours extensively interrogated. The FBI concluded in the end that she was not a spy, but merely a left-wing activist. The last report in the files, which number 750 pages in all, dates from 1973 and deals with her protests against the Vietnam War. Regina Wender died of cancer in 1997.

The Hungarian mathematician Paul Nemenyi, who was employed in the 1940s at the university of Chicago, is also mentioned in the files. He is recorded as paying a regular amount as child support for Bobby. Although that is not expanded on in the files, they seem to have suspected that he might be the real father of Bobby Fischer. Nemenyi passed away in 1952.

Bobby's sister, Joan Targ, has also died. She was felled by a brain haemorrhage on 8 June 1998. She was 60 years old. As well as her husband Russell Targ, she left three children behind: Alexander, Nicolas and Elizabeth. Elizabeth became a well-known professor of psychology at the University of California. She studied the healing power of prayer for the severely ill. Elizabeth F Targ died on 18 July 2002 as a result of a brain tumour. She was just 40.

Appendix 3

ANALYSES

Jaap van den Herik

Jaap van den Herik (born 1947) was a good chess player and an even better student of mathematics in his younger years. He can look back from the 21st century on a productive life in which both of his talents take a central place; and knowing him, there is still a lot to come. He received his PhD after in 1983 for his thesis on 'Computer Chess, the Chess World and Artificial Intelligence'. In 1987 he was appointed professor of informatics at the University of Maastricht, and since 1988 has also been a visiting professor of juridical informatics at the University of Leiden. He has continued the pioneering work of Max Euwe in artificial intelligence.

Van den Herik is the driving force behind the International Computer Games Association (ICGA), in which all board games are analyzed by computer. Most 'mind' games, such as draughts and backgammon, the modern version of the centuries-old trick-track, have been solved by this method.The computer still has big problems arriving at the 'best' move in Scrabble. Since 1990, however, computers have been a redoubtable opponent of the world's top chess players, and an excellent teacher for chess students at every level. In order to keep close track of international developments in mind-game programs, an annual world championship is organized. The University of Maastricht has been its host for the past three years.

In 1991 Van den Herik gave a speech in Leiden, underlining his respect for the potential of artificial intelligence by titling it 'Can Computers Administer Justice?' He proposed that the big backlog of legal cases, and the bitter inequality in sentences between countries, and even between regions in the same country, cry out for a digital judge. Van den Herik expects that this process will have found its way into the judicial system by around 2080.

In 2000, he began conducting research into the question of whether computers are better at attributing paintings to artists than art historians.

WHAT IS GENIUS?

Jaap van den Herik, University of Maastricht

An Unprecedented Boom

The Spassky–Fischer match, held in Reykjavik in 1972, caused an unprecedented boom in chess playing in the Netherlands. Chess was front-page news for weeks, and all chess boards were sold out even in the far corners of the countryside. Everyone was playing chess, or felt they had to learn or wanted to understand the power of the Bishops' pair. This applied to men, women and children, in fact to everything: matchboxes, light bulbs and computers should – if they were capable of doing so – play chess. The chess rage was like a virus; if you didn't play, you didn't count. It was the second (chess) boom that the Netherlands had known; in 1935, the country had been captivated by the Alekhine–Euwe World Championship match, but this time it was more serious, more comprehensive and further-reaching. This was due to the more advanced technology, because communication was up-to-the-minute, and the match could be followed live everywhere. In Amsterdam, Donner created a furore with his analysis of the games in the Psychological Laboratory, and on television, Euwe and Muhring did the same. It was clear that we were at the threshold of a new era. Chess players thought that this would be the new Fischer era, but Euwe knew better: 'Computers have arrived on earth and will never disappear again.' He said this with conviction, even then, whenever he was asked about the connection between chess and technology.

Interest in Computer Chess

The Fischer era would only last three years, and actually not even that long. Fischer hardly played serious chess at all after his victory over Spassky. Not that he lost his interest in the game; he just did not get round to it. Fischer looked further ahead, to the capabilities of computers. The question of whether a computer would be able to play had already been asked around 1950 by Claude Shannon and Alan Turing. They thought so, but the developments progressed very slowly. In 1965, Richard Greenblatt of the Massachusetts Institute of Technology (MIT) wrote the first program that almost reasoned, titled Mac Hack VI. The program gained in credibility in 1967 when it defeated the American philosopher Hubert Dreyfus, who had stated for many years that computers could not play chess. The score was therefore 1–0 in the game of computers versus philosophy. The game was, however, a joke for real chess players.

Developments continued, and because of the boom of the Fischer match, the American Sidney Samole conceived the idea of making a commercial computer for playing chess. It sold like hot cakes, although its playing strength was wretched, the way the pieces moved over the board was incorrect, and the annotation of the moves was borrowed from a different kind of algebra. The computer's name was Chess Challenger. It was difficult for beginners to annotate the moves and then demonstrate the game at their chess club. In his hurry to be the first on the market, Sidney had mixed up the horizontal (ranks) and vertical (files) lines on the board. The usual opening: 1.e2-e4 e7-e5 2.Ng1-f3 Nb8-c6 3.Bf1-b5 (Spanish/Ruy Lopez) was mangled to: 1.5b-5d 5g-5e 2.N7a-6c N2h-3f (N stands for kNight, B for Bishop). You could also play the Sicilian: 1.5b-5d 3g-3e 2.N7a-6c 4g-4f. To give it the appearance of chess annotation, Samole transformed this so it read: 1.b5-d5 g5-e5 etc.

In the meantime, in Stockholm in 1974, the Russian program Kaissa had become the first world champion in computer chess. 'The Russians again,' Fischer undoubtedly thought. Because of poor communication, he did not have access to the program. But almost no one had that in those days, because the forerunner of today's internet, the so-called ARPA-net, existed only in the United States, and only among military and academic users. The importance of communication, however, was already very clear in the world of computer chess.

Communication was the most important incentive for Doug Penrod when he attempted to record and distribute the progress of computer chess in 1975. He therefore established the *Computer Chess NewsLetter* (CCNL). It was a brilliant idea, and was very well received when its first issue appeared. That was exactly his intention, because Penrod knew that he would not be able to support the magazine for very long. He was suffering from cancer, already at an advanced stage by the time he started the CCNL. Just before his death, he gave a large party to say goodbye to all his friends. Two issues of the CCNL appeared. That seems a little, but the second issue (1977) was very special. What's more, his work was carried on by the ICCA (International Computer Chess Association), established in 1977, which started publishing its own newsletter.

Bobby Fischer was among those who received and read a copy of the first CCNL. He showed interest in computer chess and technology by writing a letter. Fischer wrote about the Chess Challenger, and about his games against Mac Hack VI. He said that he was enclosing three of the games, and gave permission to publish them. Penrod published the letter and two of the games in CCNL issue 2. Nobody knows what happened to the third game.

A Move of Genius

Among the best chess players of past and present, a few great champions stand out. Fischer is undoubtedly one of them. The question is which of these champions can also be called a *genius*. For that we would need a definition of the concept of 'genius'. Let's approach the question in a logical manner. Chess players create beautiful games, brilliant games, sometimes even games of genius. A player who plays such a game is called a genius. When Fischer was once asked what was the most brilliant move he had ever played, he answered: '17... Bg4-e6, in the game Donald Byrne–Fischer, eighth round, third Rosenwald Memorial tournament, October 1956'(see diagram 1).

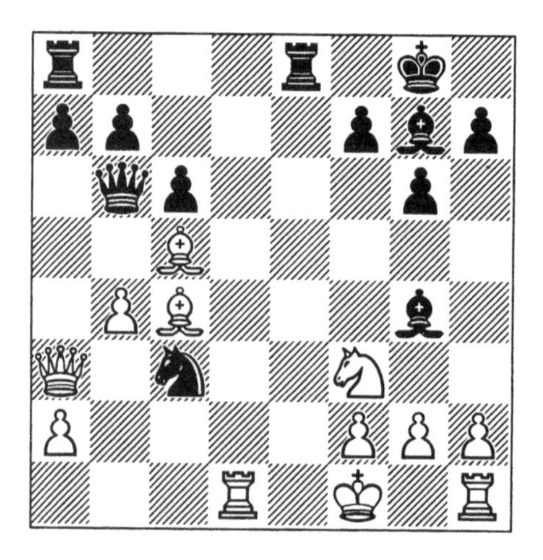

Diagram 1: position after 17.Ke1-f1

Whether that move is really a move of genius, I do not know. I would dearly like to refer to analyses in books about Fischer. (The main variation is: 18.Bxb6 Bxc4+ 19.Kg1 Ne2+ 20.Kf1 Nxd4+ 21.Kg1 Ne2+ 22.Kf1 Nc3+ 23.Kg1 axb6 etc.). The concept of genius seems to have grown in value considerably since 1956, and especially since Chess Challenger came on the scene in 1975, for if the move 17 ... Be6 is indeed a move of genius, and if this character trait may then be attributed to the person conceiving such a move, then all chess computers for sale nowadays belong to that category. They hardly need to think about this move. It is the *only* obvious move that averts all catastrophes in the position. Does that mean that the average computer is a genius? They produce in any case a move that stunned the world fifty years ago and announced the arrival of Robert J. Fischer.

Home Industry

Kasparov is a man of this day and age. He uses the computer a lot in his home analyses. That is very wise. Botvinnik too was in his time a man of the world. He spent a lot of time in opening preparation and preferred to leave nothing to chance. He had prepared himself meticulously for his meeting with Fischer (at Varna, 1962), though without a computer. Computers were not yet so strong in chess, and they were also very slow. A lot was at stake for Botvinnik: his name, his fame and his honour. He was then world champion, while Fischer belonged to the upcoming youth; he had yet to fight his way up. The game they played does indeed have the look of a clash of the titans. Botvinnik played a variation he had meticulously prepared, and by 17.e4-e5 he introduced a novelty (previously prepared for his match with Smyslov). He expected that it would bring him victory (see diagram 2).

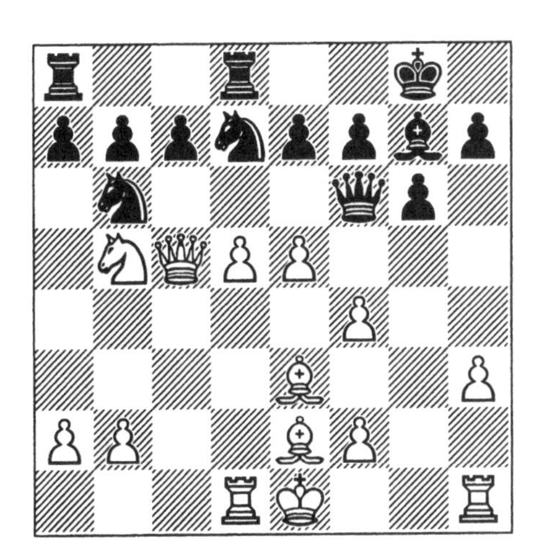

Diagram 2: position after 17.e4-e5

Fischer looked at this move and immediately found its refutation over the board: 17 ...Qf6xf4. Botvinnik must have shuddered with misery. He deserves credit for holding his own and playing on. The fight became legendary as a result of this attitude. The reader must understand, of course, that none of today's computers would have any difficulty in finding the move 17 ...Qf6xf4.They execute that move even quicker than Fischer could think of it.

The ICCA Journal

Doug Penrod's idea was thus continued by the ICCA. Ben Mittman took charge as editor of the *ICCA Newsletter* in 1977, continuing until 1983. He then asked me if I wanted to succeed him.The Technical University of Delft, my then employer, considered it a good idea, provided that I would turn it into a 'real' scientific journal. I promised to do that, and I decided to follow the example of Doug Penrod.

I therefore wrote to Professor M M Botvinnik, requesting him to contribute an article for the first issue of the *ICCA Journal*. I was overjoyed when, a few weeks later through the Soviet embassy, I received an article entitled 'The Game of Chess: its Past, Present and Future', by Botvinnik. Upon receipt of that article, I understood what Doug Penrod must have felt when he received that letter from Bobby Fischer.

Something remarkable happened then. The *ICCA Journal* held the copyright on the articles it published, something that was also clearly mentioned on the cover.That did not prevent the article being reprinted in many chess magazines around the world without my ever being asked permission. But I am happy to say that the source was often quoted. I therefore decided to let it go.

When I now reread Fischer's letter, I notice that he explicitly draws attention to the copyright. He was of the opinion that the copyright of played games should belong to the players, and that reporters should not be allowed to make unrestricted used of it. Fischer has Professor Schuijt as a partisan for this principle in the juridical world, and in the chess world he was supported by Lodewijk Prins.The ownership on the notation of a chess game was once the subject of an essay by Gerard Wildschut.The question of intellectual property rights appears to be outdated with the arrival of computers and internet communication.

Computer analysis

Computers often broke their teeth in bits and bytes on Fischer's games over the years, so there is a lot of applause for the man's genius – but sometimes a real improvement was found. We give an illustrative example of this below. As we said above, Botvinnik did not permit Fischer to push him off the board in 1962. In the end, he managed to reach the adjourned position we see in diagram 3.

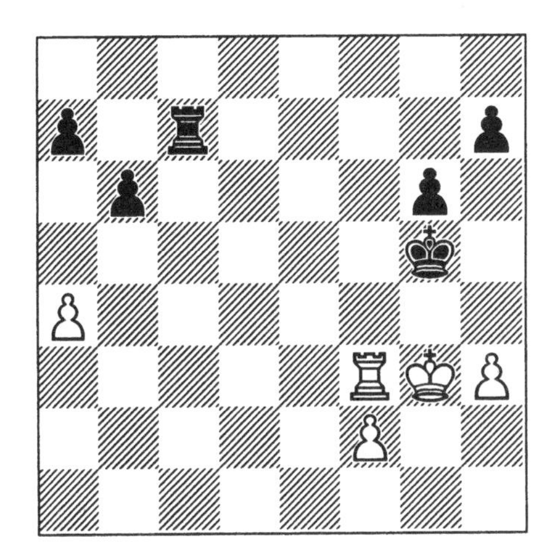

Diagram 3: position after 45.a4

The question is whether this position was won or not for Fischer. A lot depended on the sealed move. That turned out to be 45 ... Rc5. This move had been widely predicted by Botvinnik's team, who split into two groups, each of which analyzed a separate complex of variations. The game was finally drawn. Three world champions analyzed this position extensively: Botvinnik, Fischer and Kasparov. None of them was able to find a convincing winning variation.

In 1998, the chess analyst Jan van Reek had the idea that the move 45 ...Rc5 might be an incorrect one and might better have been replaced by 45 ... h5. He started to analyze the position with the help of computers. The computers available to him then, however, were not yet fast enough (and therefore not strong enough) to analyze the ramifications of this position. Just two years later the situation had significantly improved. We render below an analysis as published in the *ICCA Journal* by Van Reek, Uiterwijk and Van den Herik.

The analysis starts with *consolidation* of Black's advantage:

45. … h5!! 46.h4+ Kh6 47.Rf4 Rc5! 48.Rd4 Ra5 (both wings have now been completely consolidated.) The main variation is as follows: **49.f4** (Prevents 49. … g5) **49. … Kg7** (Start of the strategic concept of *restriction*.) **50.Kf3 Kf6 51.Ke4 Ke6 52.Rc4 Rc5 53.Rb4 Ke7! 54.Kd3 Kf6 55.Ke4 Ke6 56.Rd4 a5! 57.Ke3 Rc3+ 58.Ke4 Rb3 59.Rc4 Rb4** and Black wins.

Conclusion

Some publications have suggested that Fischer plays regularly under an alias on the internet. I do not exclude that possibility, but it goes too far simply to look at his style and attribute games to him strictly on that basis. It is however clear that Fischer possessed a lucid and clear chess style. His game distinguished itself from other grandmasters. We remark in this context that the playing style of computers differs completely from a human style. From a philosophical viewpoint, we can even postulate that computers play an entirely different game. That other game only corresponds in the outcome of the moves with the chess we humans play. That makes the meeting between human and computer so interesting. Fischer understood that, and Kramnik and Kasparov experienced it. After the matches of Deep Fritz–Kramnik 4–4 (2002) and Deep Junior–Kasparov 3–3 (2003) it is clear that computers can play at the level of Fischer. The question remains whether we call that genius. I would say: it is another form of genius.

MATCH, 1992

Fischer–Spassky

Game 1 Spanish Opening

1.e4

Even though Fischer had given a press conference, all the conditions were in accordance with his demands, and Spassky was sitting ready behind the black pieces, it was still a relief when Robert James Fischer physically made his first move. Because you never know. The book *Bobby Fischer: From Chess Genius to Legend* by Eduard Gufeld did not come out for nothing in 2002.

1…, e5 2.Nf3,Nc6 3.Bb5,a6 4.Ba4

In the 16th game of the match in 1972, Fischer, who was then leading by 9 to 6, chose the exchange variation with 4.Bxc6. The drawing-margin is then a bit bigger than in the classic patterns. After 4.Bxc6,dxc6 5.0-0,f6 6.d4,Bg4 7.dxe5,Qxd1 8.Rxd1,fxe5 9.Rd3 White is slightly better according to Fischer.

4…, Nf6 5.0-0,Be7

The classical set-up of the Spanish Opening, as Golombek's *Chess Encyclopedia* indicates, found its origin in 1490 in Lucena, and forms the absolute basis of our current chess theory. It was only in 1560 that Ruy Lopez tested this opening in practice. Therefore the Spanish is called 'Ruy Lopez' in some countries. It is – together with the Sicilian – the most frequently played opening.

6.Re1,b5 7.Bb3,d6

Spassky used in Santa Monica 1966 the Marshall defence against Fischer: 7…,0-0 8.c3,d5 9.exd5,Nxd5 10.Nxe5,Nxe5 11.Rxe5,c6 12.g3,Nf6 13.d4,Bd6 14.Re1,Bg4 with an active game for the sacrificed pawn.

8.c3,0-0 9.h3,Nb8

During the Chess Olympics in Havana in 1966, Spassky played against Fischer: 9…,h6 10.d4,Re8 11.Nbd2,Bf8 12.Nf1,Bd7 13.Ng3,Na5 14.Bc2,c5 15.b3,cxd4 16.cxd4,Nc6 17.Bb2 and White is slightly better.

10.d4,Nbd7 11.Nbd2,Bb7 12.Bc2,Re8 13.Nf1

In the 10th game in Reykjavik 1972, Fischer started a direct action on the Queen's wing with 13.b4,Bf8 14.a4. Later, Black tried many possibilities in practice in this interesting position: 14…,Nb6; 14…,c5;

14…,d5; 14…,a5. A world champion determines in his era the style in which it is played. Under Fischer that was fighting chess, under Karpov positional chess, and under Kasparov dynamic chess.

13…,Bf8 14.Ng3,g6 15.Bg5,h6 16.Bd2,Bg7 17.a4,c5 18.d5,c4

The centre is fixed, and White has to decide on which wing he will attack. Black will wait, because the only push to affect the centre, with f7-f5, is for the moment impossible.

19.b4,Nh7

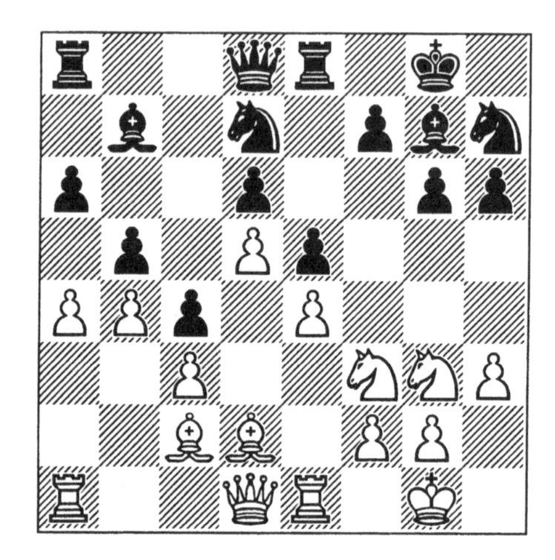

It is for the time being difficult to see how White can make progress now that the b-, c-, d-, and e-files are all closed. Maybe Spassky should have chosen to play on the Queen's wing with 19…,cxb3e.p. 20.Bxb3,Nc5 21.Bc2,Qd7, after which the e-Rook can start taking part in the game on c8 or b8. Black commits himself to waiting with the textbook move.

20.Be3,h5

In *New In Chess* 1992, grandmasters Balashov and Nikitin analyzed this game, and they ask us here to consider a different structure with Rb8, Bc8, Ndf6, Rf8, Ne8-c7, although they think that the position is 'in general favourable for White'. It then does not matter whether you play something else, one would say. 20…,h5 does not look like a lost move in any case, because White can force that push with Qd2.

21.Qd2,Rf8 22.Ra3!

Typically Fischer! It will be clear in a few moves what the idea behind Ra3 is and only then will you think: yes, indeed. You would expect White to do something against the thematic f7-f5 after which the Bishop on b7 comes to life. But Fischer has observed sharply that that push also has its downside: 22.Ra3,h4 23.Nf1,f5 24.exf5,gxf5 25.Nxg5,Nxg5 26.Bxg5,Bf6 27.Bh6,Bg7 28.Bxg7,Kxg7 29.f4,e4 30.Ne3 and White has a couple of weaknesses he can aim his arrows at. The black King is exposed. In view of the way the game is heading, Black should seriously look at this option (30…,Qf6); he has after all the half-open g-file, and the pawn on d5 does not need to be defended. Anyway, 22.Ra3 is the beginning of a crystal-clear and almost humorous regrouping.

22…,Ndf6 23.Rea1,Qd7 24.R1a2,Rfc8 25.Qc1,Bf8 26.Qa1

Triple mission accomplished. Since White has chosen the Queen's wing for its attack, he brings all his pieces to the only file that he can open, whenever it is his pleasure.

26…Qe8

So that a8 is also covered three times. If White now would exchange everything, starting with axb5, then Black can easily defend his weaknesses on b5 and d6. So Fischer first brings another piece to the Queen's wing.

27.Nf1!

This Knight wants to jump via d2 and b1 quickly to a3 in order to attack b5. The Knight on g3 was the only inefficient piece, because of Black's pawn structure. The other Knight on f3 stops all counterplay on the King's wing in the meantime.

27…,Be7 28.N1d2,Kg7 29.Nb1

And White stands ready for the multiple exchange on b5 and a8, followed by the winning Na3. Black had to do something. To give up the a-file by playing Rb8 is no option. Spassky chooses for the best defence: the Attack.

29….,Nxe4!?

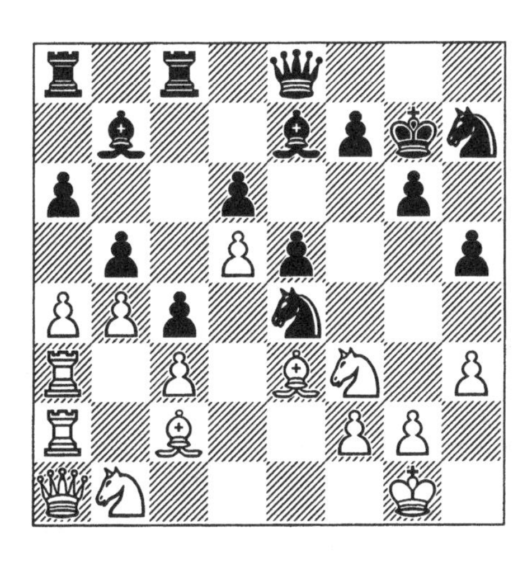

Born from need, and at the right moment now that all the white pieces stand in the corner. It does not happen often that the first piece is not captured until move 29. Black cannot wait meekly any longer, because the intelligently structured invasion over the a-file would increase the overall pressure on the black position.

30.Bxe4,f5

Spassky could have captured a second pawn also in another way. With Nf6 the weakly positioned Knight gets going again: 31...,Nf6 32.Bc2,Nxd5 33.axb5,axb5 34.Rxa8,Rxa8 35.Rxa8,Qxa8 36.Qxa8,Bxa8 37.Ba7,f5 and Black has all the central squares. Or 33.Bd2,f5 34.axb5,axb5 35.Ra7,Rxa7 36.Rxa7,Ra8 37.Qa5,Rxa7 38.Qxa7,Qa8 39.Qxa8,Bxa8 40.Bg5,Bxg5 41.Nxg5,Kf6 42.h4,Bc6 then how would White invade or break in? White is of course better in all these kinds of positions and Black gets a long and rough massage, but this move 30...,Nf6 also gives him a good chance to defend himself.

31.Bc2,Bxd5 32.axb5,axb5

Here 33.Rxa8,Rxa8 34.Rxa8,Qxa8 35.Na3,Bc6 would not create problems for Black. His pawn front does not show any weaknesses and prevents all entries.

33.Ra7,Kf6?!

In any case an interesting move. The black King withdraws from the pinning attack and takes part in the game just in case all black pieces are exchanged. Still, the advanced position of the King provides new attacking chances, as will soon become apparent. The normal continuation deserves therefore the preferable play: 33...,Rxa7 34.Rxa7,Ra8 35.Nbd2,Rxa7 36.Qxa7,Bc6 with the intention of playing Qd7.

Remarkably enough, Balashov and Nikitin give 33...,Kf6! and state: 'Protected by his pawns, the King stands here safer than after the sad 33...,Kg8.'

34.N1d2

White has the a-file and manoeuvres back to the King's wing.

34...,Rxa7 35.Rxa7,Ra8

With the intention of playing Rxa7 and the exchange of Queens by Qa8 after which White – despite his material advantage – will have difficulty in making progress. Little can be done against it. White has to be fast if he wants to win in the attack. How will Fischer create a new attacking plan?

36.g4!

See the commentary at move 30 and 33. Spassky is to be excused that he overlooked this brilliant sacrificial break in his advance calculation.

36....,hxg4 37.hxg4,Rxa7

Black is in difficulties. 37...,Ke6 indeed prevents Nh4 but it does not solve all problems: 37...,Ke6 38.Qb1,Qf8 39.Rxa8,Bxa8 and White still has play, e.g. 40.Qf1 with the threat Qh3 (on 40.Qf1,fxg4 41.Nh2,Nf6 42.Qe2.)

38.Qxa7,f4

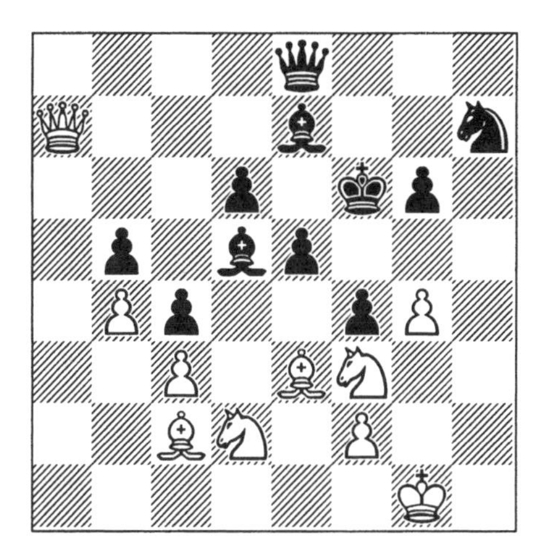

According to the analysis of Balashov and Nikitin, this is the first mistake in the game. They judge: 'After 38...,f4? Spassky omits maintaining the tension and makes a move that changes the black pawn structure into a ruin. After 38...,Be6!, with the intention of Qd7, the continuation of the game would have been difficult to predict.'

These kinds of pronouncements are not in general appropriate in a solid analysis (it is saying, in effect, 'reader, you figure it out yourself!'). But in the analysis of a historic game in a trade journal, they are frankly annoying.

The position is pre-eminently suitable as study material. But what is the position really like? Is White winning or not? Let's add a few more logical moves from that analysis in *New In Chess* 1992. 38...,Be6 39.Nh4,Qd7 40.Qa8,Qc8 41.Qf3! White's attack is dangerous with the Queens on the board. To give an example: 41...,Qd7 42.Ne4+,Kg7 43.gxf5,gxf5 44.Qg3+ and White will win. Since Black cannot play (after 39.Nh4) any of the following moves: g5, fxg4, f4, e4, or d5, the King is stuck defending square f5; the Queen must defend Be7 (If 39...,Qc8 then 40.Nxg6.) and White starts the deadly attack with the switch Qa7-b7-f3 if Black does not do anything. The assessment of this position should therefore be not 'difficult to predict' but 'White is winning'.

Spassky of course expected the normal 39.Bb6, a move quite a few world champions would have played because White continues to be better and can keep the pressure on for a long time without danger of losing. Black then has two choices, of which the best is: 39.Bb6,Qa8 40.Qxa8,Bxa8 41.Ne4+,Ke6 42.Nfd2,Bb7. Black remains passive and only plays d5 when the Knight cannot jump to c5. The other choice looks more active: 39.Bb6,Qc6 and Black threatens along the long diagonal. That threat is, however, only apparent, in view of 40.Bd8,Bxd8 41.Qxh7,Bxf3 42.Qh8+ and White wins.

As is clear from all the above ways to play for Black, the best defence in this difficult and slightly lesser position is total passivity. Spassky tries – completely justifiably just before the time-control – 38…,f4 because he is lost anyway and the refutation is not easy to find.

39.Bxf4!

Hits the nail on the head. The pawn defence around the King is blown up. It requires a great deal of self-confidence to change on the 39th move a generally better position with material advantage into a position in which you end up behind in material. All the more so because a couple of special moves have to follow.

39…,exf4

The intermediate move 39…,Bxf3 cannot be considered: 40.Bxe5+,dxe5 41.Nxf3,Qc6 42.g5+,Ke6 43.Qe3,Qd5 44.Bxg6,Nf8 45.Be4.

40.Nh4!

And not even a quick check to reach the time-control, because after 40.Qd4+,Ke6 square h4 is inaccessible. White of course can then also continue with 41.Qxf4,Kd7 42.Qh6 and the g-pawn falls, but the textbook move is much more compelling.

40….,Bf7

The time-control has been reached, Black is a pawn up but his position is a straight loss. Fischer finishes in style.

41.Qd4+,Ke6

A beautiful mate would follow after: 41…,Kg5 42.Qg7,Nf6 43.Nhf3+,Kxg4 44.Qh6,Nh5 45.Nh2+,Kh4 46.Ndf3+,Kh3 47.Qxh5+,gxh5 48.Bf5+.

42.Nf5!,Bf8

42…,Kd7 is not possible because of 43.Qa7+,Kd8 44.Qb8+,Kd7 45.Qxb5+,Kd8 46.Qb8+,Kd7 47.Ba4+.

43.Qxf4,Kd7

A technical won position remains after 43...,gxf5 44.Bxf5+,Ke7 45.Bxh7.

44.Nd4,Qe1+

The chess of vengeance, as the expression goes. The b-pawn was attacked and 44...,Kc7 45.Nxb5+,Qxb5 46.Qxf7 does not help.

45.Kg2,Bd5+ 46.Be4,Bxe4 47.Nxe4

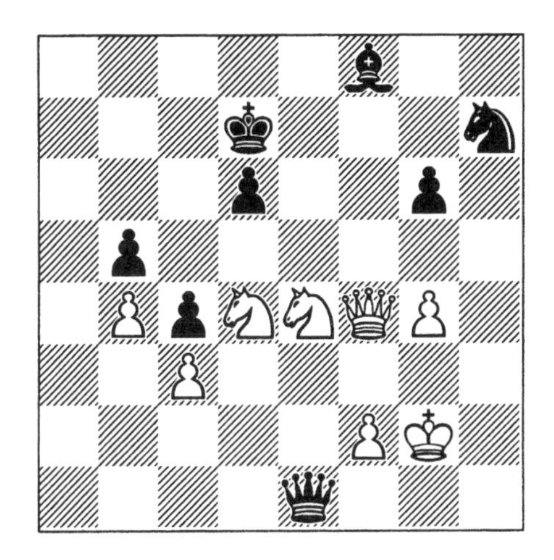

The position is, just like the initial position, in a completely material equilibrium, but all white pieces stand in overpowering positions while all black pieces are inactive. This is the crowning of the entire white strategy. The position is a joy to behold.

47...,Be7 48.Nxb5,Nf8

The Knight still tramples a bit in its death-struggle.

49.Nbxd6,Ne6 50.Qe5

and because of a lack of sensible moves Black resigns.

This trial of strength adorns both the winner and the loser. Spassky landed in a lesser position without making any apparent errors. He forces his opponent to resort to fantasy and promptness of action by 29...,Nxe4. That strategy would have sufficed against many an opponent. But not against Robert James Fischer. The latter played impressively: a captivating opening with potential threats on both wings, a harmonious transition to the middle game initiated with 22.Ra3, repulsion of every counter-play, creative reaction to a speculative sacrifice, hit at exactly the right time with a counter-sacrifice, and finally a faultless simplification to victory. Fischer did not make a single lesser move.

This was an errorless game by White, and that does not happen very often. Historically, that has never been known to occur for someone who had not played a serious game for 20 years. What a delightful chess fight!

Appendix 4

FISCHER IN JAIL

by Kaarlo Schepel

Not just the world of chess but all Americans were amazed to discover on 16 July 2004 that the former world chess champion Bobby Fischer – now 61 – had been detained by immigration authorities in Japan. A spokesman at Tokyo's Narita Airport said Fischer was stopped on Tuesday 13 July while trying to leave Japan for the Philippines. A Japanese newspaper said officials were preparing to deport Fischer to the United States, where he was wanted for travelling to Yugoslavia in 1992 to play a match against another former champion, Boris Spassky. The US authorities said that trip violated UN sanctions against Yugoslavia. The US Embassy in Tokyo would only say that it was aware Fischer had been detained. Apparently, Fischer (a big man, certainly by Japanese standards) put up a vigorous fight and had to be physically restrained by several officials. He was certainly injured in the fight, losing at least one tooth. The events following his arrest up to the date of publication can be followed on his own website at http://home.att.ne.jp/moon/fischer/list/p_52/52_0.htm, which includes the following message:

'The World Chess Champion Bobby Fischer has been viciously attacked brutalized seriously injured and very nearly killed when he was illegally detained and arrested by the Japanese immigration authorities at Narita international airport in Tokyo Japan. They illegally detained Bobby Fischer at the Narita airport jailhouse. Furthermore in collusion with the US government the Japanese immigration authorities have confiscated and destroyed Bobby Fischer's US passport. Bobby Fischer is still in jail at Narita airport in Tokyo Japan. Bobby Fischer does not wish to return to the Jew-controlled USA where he faces a kangaroo court and 10 years in Federal prison and a likely early demise or worse on trumped political charges. Nor does he wish to remain in a hostile brutal and corrupt US-controlled Japan. He urgently requests an immediate offer of political asylum from a friendly third country. Any country wishing to offer Bobby Fischer political asylum should do so immediately at the following address: Miyoko Watai Japan Chess Association [...] This is a matter of life and death for Bobby. Thank you!'

Chess friends from the United States contacted Japan on 16 July. They heard confirmation of the arrest from Miss Watai, Secretary of the Japan Chess Association. She had been its acting head since the death of its president, Yasuji Matsumoto, in 2003. Both were known to have been friendly with Bobby Fischer since his first visits to Tokyo in 1976–77. Miyoko Watai had herself played in many Olympiad teams for Japan.

The basis for his detention appeared to be that the US Embassy in Manila had sent a letter via US Consul General Theodore Arega informing the Japanese authorities that Bobby Fischer's passport had been revoked. The letter was dated 11 December 2003 but Bobby Fischer had not received the letter, and did not know about it.

The letter states that Bobby Fischer's US Passport was revoked pursuant to Section 51.70(a) of Title 22 of the Code of Federal Regulations, in that Fischer was charged with violating 50 USC 1701, 1702 and 1705 on December 15, 1992. These are provisions that gives the US president the authority to deal with any unusual or extraordinary threat to National Security (further legal details can be found at http://caselaw.lp.findlaw.com/scripts/ts_search.pl?title=50&sec=1701 and http://caselaw.lp.findlaw.com/casecode/uscodes/50/chapters/35/sections/section_1702.html).

The next two weeks saw vigorous debates on various internet chess chat groups and forums, in which those who detest Fischer because of his political views applauded the fact that US authorities had finally acted. Others decried the action, saying that freedom of expression is a constitutional right, and that this was cheap, election-year politics. Some chess players and members of the American Federation (USCF) pointed out that the USCF had been the biggest beneficiary of Fischer's career of any party. Seemingly single-handed, Fischer had quadrupled the membership of the USCF in the years leading up to his reign from 1972–75 . The USCF had, however, decided to strip Fischer of his life membership after 9/11. Appropriate words were said about fair-weather friendships. And of course a few correspondents applauded his arrest on the grounds that he could finally get 'help' for his mental illness. But the harsh words Fischer had spoken on the very day of 11 September stuck in the mind of most American chess players.

A number of old friends were not afraid to defend Fischer, however. Redoubtable internet journalist and publisher Sam Sloan (a boyhood chess friend of Fischer and himself known for his travels, websites and controversial views) wrote immediately: 'Fischer never used the words "World Trade Center" in his recorded comments on 9/11. He spent almost the entire broadcast talking about the Palestinian issue. Since this was broadcast in the Philippines, which is 13 hours ahead of the US, and Fischer was in Japan, which is 14 hours ahead of the US, and since the World Trade Center did not fall down until after 10:00 am, by which time it was 9/12 in Japan, plus the fact that this was broadcast on 9/11 Japan or Philippines time, plus the fact that the interviewer made no mention of the collapse of the World Trade Center, all points to the conclusion that the World Trade Center had not fallen at the time that Fischer spoke these words, so he could not have known about the tremendous loss of life that subsequently resulted.'

Immediate past USCF President John McCrary recalled on a forum that 'If memory serves, [old friend] Leland Fuerstman of North Carolina had been in touch with Fischer around that time to try to induce his return. He got his Congressman to introduce this resolution, which passed routinely in the House, as a condition put forth by Fischer. However, the USCF Delegates that year refused to do the same. I think Fuerstman also tried that year, also unsuccessfully, to get the Delegates to provide Fischer's dental insurance, or some such benefit.'

Bobby Fischer's former brother-in-law stated that this is presidential electoral politics. Others commented that 'Some guy in the Justice Department (with approval of Ashcroft) decided that Bobby Fischer was a perfect scapegoat. His views are detested by over 90% of the American population. It may assure the administration of a large part of the Jewish vote. Bobby Fischer may be sick, but he is being used as a pawn.'

In the meantime, Fischer's passport was destroyed by the US Embassy in Tokyo. His extradition is postponed at the time of writing, pending legal procedures, and Fischer officially states on his website and through his lawyer that he is renouncing his US nationality. He appeals to countries worldwide to give him asylum, notably Germany as his (official, not biological) father had that nationality. A 'Free Bobby' website has been set up where people can vote for him, and find email addresses of just about anyone (including President Bush) that might be in a position to get him out of jail and stop extradition.

His old friend IM Dimitrije Bjelica of Serbia-Montenegro says he has found a sponsor to play a four-game match in his prison cell (the prize money exceeding the Reykjavik fund of $250,000). Many journalists have also ridiculed the jailing of someone who has never physically hurt a fly. In the words of former US Chess Life editor Larry Parr:

'I have no idea whether Bush *fils* even knows the name of Bobby Fischer. I do know that the issue is not whether Fischer broke a federal law (he must have, and so have all of us) but whether he is a criminal as opposed to someone who has fallen afoul of the federal regime. Americans have been largely sold on the State as the new god. There was a time when juries did not take a judge's instructions as gospel and rendered verdicts based on natural law suppositions. In 19th century England, juries would not convict for minor theft no matter what the proof happened to be because the punishment in many instances – hanging – was utterly disproportionate to the crime.'

Bobby played chess, practiced his art. He is being held in jail for doing this – not for stealing your wallet, not for raping someone's daughter, not for gunning down his next door neighbour, not for defrauding anyone. His act of playing chess became criminal because George Bush *père* issued an executive order.

On 21 August 2004, the Associated Press reported:

'A Japanese court dismissed a request to halt deportation proceedings against fugitive chess legend Bobby Fischer, his lawyers said.... The Tokyo District Court rejected the request to have Japanese immigration officials halt procedures to deport him, his legal team said in a faxed statement. Fischer's lawyers immediately filed an appeal with the Tokyo High Court, saying the decision was unjust and unreasonable. Earlier in the day, Fischer's lead lawyer, Masako Suzuki, had predicted such an outcome and filed a separate request to the justice ministry, asking that Fischer not be immediately deported if there was an unfavourable court decision. Suzuki argued that immediate deportation would violate Fischer's right to a fair trial, according to an earlier faxed copy of the request. The request also said Fischer, 61, should be allowed to stay in Japan on humanitarian grounds, citing his plans to marry a Japanese woman. Earlier this week, Miyoko Watai (59), head of the Japan Chess Association, announced that she and Fischer were engaged. Watai denied the engagement was intended to influence the deportation proceedings. Fischer has fought deportation since being detained July 13 by attempting to seek political asylum in Japan or a third country, as well as renouncing his US citizenship.'

Fischer's old friend and US chess legend GM Larry Evans (himself now detested by Fischer) writes the following in US Chess Life (November 2004) in his Readers Mailbag column in answer to a question on the failed 1975 title fight:

'Most readers agreed with me, but some took me to task for not backing Bobby because he was my friend and a fellow American. The Soviets quoted me to prove that even a close aide didn't support his absurd demands. 'To play until 10 victories is awful,' said Karpov. 'The match can last 3 or 4 months ... [it would] cease being an art and turn into forced labour. That would be a marathon which would risk my health and sanity.'

Louis Statham, whose annual tournament at Lone Pine was world famous, summed up the view of many fans: 'I think it's unworthy for a champion of anything to ask for a handicap.' Even Ayn Rand chimed in: 'Fischer throws tantrums like a child, breaks agreements, makes arbitrary demands, and indulges in behaviour that would disqualify him for a high school tournament.'

In 'Will Fischer Win the Endgame of his Life?' (online at http://tinyurl.com/6pf2w) I noted: 'Before Bobby won the title, he demanded that the challenger (himself) should have absolutely fair conditions, and he objected to Spassky having draws odds in 24 games. In this he was right. His later behaviour was outrageous, and nobody knows whether he would have played even if FIDE had given him everything he wanted. I agree with what Kasparov wrote recently in The Wall Street Journal: "Fischer demolished the Soviet chess machine but could build nothing in its place. He was an ideal challenger – but a disastrous champion."

'I tried to persuade Bobby to set a shining example by renouncing any advantage. "But you didn't think the champ should have any edge when you were the challenger,' I argued. 'That's besides the point! The Russkies always made the rules and got away with it. Let's give 'em a dose of their own medicine," he replied. He promised not to seek any edge in future matches if he got his way just this once. Reasoning with him was futile. I don't think he ever quite forgave me for trying to get him to do the right thing.

'... He insisted only 10 wins should count – not draws – which might take forever by turning into a marathon. What stuck in everyone's craw and what did lead to his forfeiting the FIDE title was his demand to stop the match at a 9–9 tie with the purse divided evenly and the champion keeping the title. This provision meant Karpov had to win by at least two points (10–8).... Pal Benkö alleged that Bobby feared the Russians would have him killed if he played Karpov. Whatever the reason – real or imagined – not defending his title was a tragedy for Bobby and a tragedy for chess. Sadly, his selfmate handed the title back to the Soviets without a fight.

'At Caracas in 1977, FIDE accepted Bobby's principle that only wins should count and decreed the title would go to the player who first won six games in an open-ended match. But they gave Karpov a rematch clause, a bigger edge than Bobby ever sought. Bobby was furious. He vowed to get even and finally imposed his rules in the $5 million duel with Spassky in 1992. This match was played outside of FIDE's jurisdiction and billed as "The Return Match of the Century Between the Never Defeated Champion of the World and His Challenger Boris Spassky".